MENTORING
PROGRAMS FOR
NEW TEACHERS

MENTORING
PROGRAMS FOR
NEW TEACHERS

Models of Induction and Support

SUSAN VILLANI

Foreword by Charlotte Danielson

CORWIN PRESS, INC.
A Sage Publications Company
Thousand Oaks, California

Copyright © 2002 by Corwin Press, Inc.

For information:

Corwin Press, Inc.
A Sage Publications Company
2455 Teller Road
Thousand Oaks, California 91320
E-mail: order@corwinpress.com

CORWIN PRESS

Sage Publications Ltd.
6 Bonhill Street
London EC2A 4PU
United Kingdom

Sage Publications India Pvt. Ltd.
M-32 Market
Greater Kailash I
New Delhi 110 048 India

Printed in the United States of America

Library of Congress Cataloging-in-Publication Data

Villani, Susan.
    Mentoring programs for new teachers: Models of induction and support / by Susan Villani.
        p. cm.
Includes bibliographical references.
    ISBN 0-7619-7868-2 (c.) — ISBN 0-7619-7869-0 (pbk.)
    1. First year teachers—In-service training—United States.
2. Mentoring in education—United States.   I. Title.
    LB2844.1.N4 V55 2002
    371.102—dc21   2001003981

This book is printed on acid-free paper.

01   02   03   04   05   06   07   7   6   5   4   3   2   1

Acquisitions Editor: Robb Clouse
Associate Editor: Kylee Liegl
Editorial Assistant: Erin Buchanan
Production Editor: Olivia Weber
Typesetter/Designer: Hespenheide Design
Cover Designer: Tracy E. Miller

Contents

Foreword:
The Need for Mentoring

The idea that beginning teachers require a structured system to support their entry into the profession has moved from the fringes of the policy landscape to the center; it is now generally recognized as a critical component of a comprehensive approach to teacher development, and is mandated in many states. As the education community develops better understanding of the life cycle of a teaching career, and of how best to support professional learning by teachers, the first few years of practice are widely acknowledged as critical steps in the development of expertise.

Teaching is the only career without a recognized apprenticeship stage. Physicians and surgeons are not asked to make diagnoses or perform operations unsupervised at the end of their classroom training—that supervision is the purpose of internships and residencies. Newly licensed architects are not asked to design a major building during their first week on the job, nor are novice attorneys given the full responsibility for a major case. But a new teacher has the same responsibilities as a veteran with 20 years' experience.

Furthermore, in many settings, beginning teachers are presented with more challenging teaching assignments than their more experienced colleagues. They are frequently assigned the most preparations, the most challenging students, and no classroom of their own. Although these practices are unconscionable, they are widespread.

It is small wonder, then, that attrition rates among new teachers are so high. Estimates vary, but most researchers maintain that about 30 percent of teachers leave the profession within the first five years, with a staggering 50 percent in urban and isolated rural areas. This represents a tremendous cost—both human and economic.

The human cost is unmistakable. Most teachers in training begin their education programs filled with optimism and confidence. Many have a strong calling to the profession, and expect to be successful. In general, that confidence lasts into their first year of teaching, when they are confronted with the daunting challenges of real students, presenting real situations. They are, in most situations, thrown into the proverbial deep end, and expected to sink or swim.

The lack of support for beginning teachers appears to be grounded in the erroneous belief that they have learned all they need to know to be successful in their preparation programs. If they are not successful, it is their own fault; they are not tough enough or not fit in some way for the rigors of teaching. The struggle is captured in the words of one first-year teacher, "My descent from innocence was swift and brutal. I was given a temporary role sheet, assigned a room—actually three different rooms—and with little other preparation was thrust into the world of teaching" (Shulman & Colbert, 1988, p. 22).

Fortunately, well-conceived induction programs have been developed to make a difference in the success rates of beginning teachers, and many of them are described in this book. Attrition rates are dropping, and teachers' skills and confidence in their work is significantly improved. When asked, "If you had the opportunity to make the decision again, would you choose teaching as a career?" far more answer in the affirmative than in the negative.

So, what makes for a well-conceived induction program? What are its elements?

1. The induction program is far more than a buddy system, in which the buddy is available as a sounding board and a sympathetic ear and shoulder. A buddy is important, and every well-designed program includes provision for a more experienced colleague to offer moral support. But well-designed programs consist of far more than buddies—they provide help with instruction as well.

2. The induction program provides more than practical guidance on school policies and procedures, such as how to order

supplies or videos, or how to conduct back-to-school night. Again, this type of assistance is important, but not sufficient.

3. The program includes more than generalized support. Coaching of a novice teacher can assist that individual in clarifying goals and exploring options. But learning to teach is a highly complex undertaking, and the novice's progress is hastened by well-designed activities focused on the improvement of practice. The program should be organized around a vision of good teaching, a common language that serves to structure the professional conversations between beginning teachers and their mentors.

4. The program includes adequate training for the mentors and orientation for the site administrators, so they can carry out their roles with skill. Ideally, the training for mentors engages them in important professional learning, and a heightened awareness of their own practice.

5. The program engages beginning teachers in self-assessment, reflection on practice, and formative assessment—the same ingredients found to enhance learning by all, students as well as adults.

6. Lastly, the program is planned and organized, with adequate resources to compensate mentors, schedule time for mentors and beginning teachers to work together, and support for the mentors (who are, after all, performing a new role). Mentoring of new teachers is not (or should not be) a haphazard affair; it must be organized for success.

The programs described in this book offer practitioners a valuable tour of the mentoring landscape. They range widely, from those that have been developed by educators in their own settings, to others that have been developed nationally and implemented in a range of locations. They vary in the amount, and type, of training for mentors, and in the type of activities used by beginning teachers. Those searching for guidance will find much to draw on here.

—*Charlotte Danielson*

Preface

Phew, I've finally finished hiring for September. For a while there, it didn't seem like we would get all the positions filled. It is definitely harder to get the qualified candidates we want for all the openings we have. There were predictions that this would happen . . . warnings of a teacher shortage . . . and now it is hitting home.

While I'm glad to have completed the hiring, a thought nags at me: We better keep all these people, because replacing them and hiring people for new positions will be even more of a problem in the next few years.

We've got to support our new staff. Many of them asked about that during their interviews. I said some vague things about orientation and ongoing assistance, but I don't really have it figured out. How will we orient them to our schools? There are so many things new teachers need to learn all at once, not to mention how much more of a learning curve it will be for the teachers who are working toward an alternative certification. Even experienced teachers who are new to our district have a lot to learn about school culture.

I wonder how our veteran staff would react to an invitation to become involved. I've heard that mentoring can have a big impact on them as well. Some people even say that mentoring can make a difference in school culture.

I don't have time to research this idea of mentoring, but I want to make an informed decision. It would help to know what is out there. Should we just find out what a neighboring school system is doing and copy it? I'd hate to commit our time, energy, and money to something that doesn't work for us. Where do I begin?

Maybe this is your concern:

I don't see how we're going to keep our mentoring program with the number of new teachers we'll be hiring this summer. It's been hard enough finding the money for mentor stipends each year, and now the number of mentors will nearly double. We've worked so hard to set up our mentoring program; I would hate to pull the plug on it now. Especially when people see such value in it. I wonder what else we could do.

All these new teachers are being hired, and there isn't any organized way to support them during the year. Some of us help one or two of them, especially if they are at our grade level or subject area. But we each do different things, and there isn't much time to really help them with their teaching. It sounds like a couple of them are really struggling, but they're afraid to tell anyone. One new teacher left in the middle of the year, and two others didn't come back this year. We need to do something!

Acknowledgments

Helen Villani, for suggesting I become a teacher, and for encouraging me to write

Pat Keohane, for giving me a chance to student-teach in her first grade classroom, and modeling caring about students' achievement and well-being

Lonnie Carton, for inspiring me as a graduate student to do the unconventional, if it meant making learning relevant to students

Laura Cooper, for defining a process to design, implement, and evaluate a mentoring program in the Concord, MA, public schools that became a reference point in my thinking

Julie Nann and Kevin Harding, for their creativity and close connection as we trained and supported mentors

Jean Latham, for telling Debbie Sherman about my work, which led to an invitation to plan and teach courses in a mentoring certificate program offered by Lesley University

Eileen McSweeny, for pairing Kathy Dunne and me to design and offer a mentoring institute through EdCo, giving me a taste of the excitement of synergistic professional development with colleagues

Kathy Dunne, for becoming my mentor when I joined Learning Innovations at WestEd, modeling consultation and facilitation at its finest, and nurturing my growth and confidence as a staff developer.

Colleagues at Learning Innovations, and Director, Jan Phlegar, for walking their talk about collaboration, positive presupposition, and mutual support of risk-taking to promote growth

Ted Britton and Senta Raizen, for sharing their abundant collection of materials on mentoring

Elizabeth Foster, for telling me about the Mentoring Symposium, (sponsored by the New Teacher Project at University of California at Santa Cruz) which was an excellent opportunity for me to network with practitioners who have established dynamic mentoring programs

Linda Spence, Janice Mays, and Micki MacGregor, for their diligent follow-up on interviews I had with their project directors, and for providing me with information and clarification of their programs

Judy Walsh, for making time, when there was none, to locate information about the New Teacher Project and sending it so promptly

Lynn Marshall, a "get it done" person at NEA, for helping me obtain reprint information even though it was not part of the work she typically does

Tony Phillips, for keeping my energy flowing during the physically taxing time of intense writing

Marlyn Miller, Kelli Fitzgerald, Anne Shaughn, and Sue Wurster for reading my manuscript and giving valuable feedback

Robb Clouse, for mentoring me into publishing with information, encouragement, enthusiasm, and trust

Henry Damon, for working with me on clarifying concepts, synthesizing ideas, and improving the introductory and concluding chapters

My family, friends, and colleagues, for encouraging me and understanding my absences to research and write

The directors of the programs described in this book, for their time, commitment to this project, enthusiasm, and contribution to the profession and so many teachers, graduate students, and other colleagues who have informed my thinking.

* * *

Corwin Press would also like to acknowledge the following reviewers:

Karen Tichy
Associate Superintendent for Instruction
Catholic Education Office
St. Louis, MO

Penelope Walter Swenson
Assistant Superintendent
Mojave Unified School District
Mojave, CA

Harriet Gould
Principal
Raymond Central Elementary School
Valparaiso, NE

J. Fred Schouten
Director of Curriculum and Technology
Peotone Community Unit District
Peotone, IL

Harry Hufty
Consultant
Allwest Research, Information, and Evaluation Services (ARIES)
Prince George, BC

About the Author

Susan Villani, Senior Program/Research Associate at Learning Innovations at WestEd, specializes in designing professional development. She leads and facilitates program design and offers mentor teacher and/or administrator training. She collaborates with schools, districts, and departments of education to tailor program offerings that address their staff development needs. Her areas of expertise include: mentoring and induction of new teachers, leadership development, diversity, and equity.

Susan is also a Senior Adjunct Faculty member for Lesley University; she teaches Dimensions of Equity and Action Research courses throughout the United States. Her commitment to the inclusion of all students, and the richness of the diverse cultural identities of every member of a school community, is a major theme in her work with graduate students, as it was when she was an elementary school principal for twenty-one years.

Susan is on the Board of the Massachusetts Association of Supervision and Curriculum Development (MASCD) and was previously on the Program Advisory Board of the Principals' Center at Harvard University. As former President of the North East Coalition of Educational Leaders (NECEL), Susan worked throughout New England to promote women in or interested in educational leadership.

Throughout her career, Susan has been most interested in working with children and adults to identify and realize their dreams. She is inspired by the turtle, which sticks its neck out to make progress.

For Jerry Villani, my father and first
coach, who saw in me things I didn't see
in myself, and who recently mentored a
96-year-old musician

&

For Henry Damon, my husband,
who has mentored administrators
and countless new teachers, including
his son Bob and daughter Kate,
my step-adults

Part 1

Contemplating the Induction of New Teachers

Mentoring New Teachers: Models of Induction and Support is a way to help you get started. It describes different models of mentoring, and gives you the information you need to get started thinking about orientation and professional support and development that will affect hiring, orientation, and teacher effectiveness, as well as staff morale. It gives you an idea of some of the ways schools, teachers' associations, institutions of higher education, educational collaboratives, and state departments of education are supporting new teachers. Its primer style makes understanding these models and comparing their relative merits doable. In just a few hours, you can begin to imagine what mentoring model might work well in your school, district, or region. After more thought and conversation with colleagues, you may even think about combining the components of several to create a unique version for yourselves.

Inducting New Teachers: Addressing Needs and Supporting Learning

Many kinds of mentoring programs exist to promote the smooth entry and heightened effectiveness of new teachers, whose numbers are rapidly expanding. The National Education Association projects that 200,000 new teachers will be hired in each of the next ten years. Other estimates suggest we will hire 2.5 million new teachers in the next decade. While you might be feeling considerable pressure to get a mentoring program started in your school system or to change to a model that better matches your resources, for long-term success you need to consider carefully what it is you want your induction of new teachers to accomplish.

For new teachers, a contract and a handshake are just the beginning. We know that new teachers must adapt well and quickly to their schools and teaching assignments, because they have students who are counting on them as soon as classes begin. Experienced teachers can do many things, formally and informally, to help new teachers learn the ropes and get off to a good start. Understanding their needs makes it possible to provide the support they require and deserve.

> Effective professional development is a design task that requires understanding the needs of the adult learners and selecting appropriate strategies to promote growth.

The Needs of New Teachers

The needs of new teachers are articulated well by Veenman (1984, pp. 153-156), who ranked the ten problems reported most frequently by new teachers: classroom discipline, student motivation, dealing with individual differences among students, assessment of student work, interaction with parents, organizing work, obtaining sufficient materials for adequate instruction, dealing with students' personal problems, heavy course loads with inadequate preparation time, and getting along with colleagues. Gordon and Maxey (2000, p. 6) have identified the following high-priority needs of beginning teachers:

- Managing the classroom
- Acquiring information about the school system
- Obtaining instructional resources and materials
- Planning, organizing, and managing instruction, as well as other professional responsibilities
- Assessing students and evaluating student progress
- Motivating students
- Using effective teaching methods
- Dealing with individual students' needs, interests, abilities, and problems
- Communicating with colleagues, including administrators, supervisors, and other teachers
- Communicating with parents
- Adjusting to the teaching environment and role
- Receiving emotional support

"Reality shock" is what Veenman called the state of mind new teachers often enter when they first deal with the demands of teaching. A study of teacher education students found they tended to believe they would experience less difficulty than the "average first-year teacher" on a number of different tasks. This study suggests that novice teachers leave pre-service programs and enter the profession believing that teaching is not particularly difficult (Weinstein, 1988). While new teachers do need to come to terms with the many requirements of teaching, it may be useful for mentors to help them anticipate the upcoming "shock."

The needs of new teachers are represented in Figure 1.1, which depicts the survival needs of new teachers as highest at the beginning

Figure 1.1. Types of Mentor Support

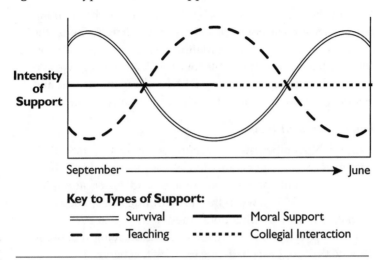

SOURCE: *Concord Public Schools Mentor Handbook,* copyright 1984, based on Veenman (1984). Adapted with permission.

and the ending of the school year, with the curriculum and instruction needs at those times being less pronounced. Conversely, midyear, when the survival needs of new teachers are lowest, their needs regarding curriculum and instruction are greatest. This makes a lot of sense. As articulated by Maslow in his hierarchy of needs construct, we cannot address higher order needs until our survival needs are satisfied. Similarly, teachers cannot be thinking about the nuances of curriculum design and instruction until they know the protocols of their school and have established that their students are engaged and ready to learn.

Five Phases Experienced by First-Year Teachers

Moir and colleagues at the New Teacher Center identified the following:

Anticipation Phase
Before teachers start their first assignment, they are idealistic, excited, and anxious.

Survival Phase

During the first month of school, the new teacher is bombarded with a variety of problems and situations he or she has not anticipated. Besides planning and preparing lessons, the new teacher is responsible for organization tasks like taking lunch counts, announcing PTA fund-raising drives, and establishing classroom routines and procedures.

Disillusionment Phase

Around November, new teachers begin to question their commitment and their competence. They are faced with Back to School Night, parent conferences, and observations by their principals. Just when they are running fast to keep pace with all the varied obligations, they need to run even faster to keep up. It is a time of distress. . . . Surviving this phase may be the toughest challenge for new teachers.

Figure 1.2. The Phases of a First-Year Teacher's Attitude Toward Teaching

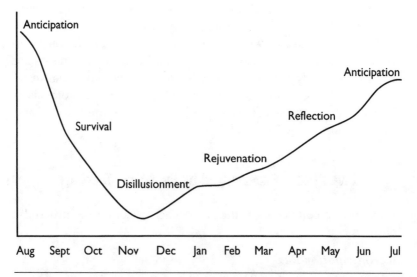

SOURCE: From "The stages of a teacher's first year" by E. Moir in *A better beginning: Supporting and mentoring new teachers*, edited by M. Schurer, copyright 1999 by the Association of Supervision and Curriculum Development. Reprinted with permission.

Rejuvenation Phase

After winter break, teachers feel rested and rejuvenated. There is a slow rise in the teacher's attitude. They come back with renewed hope and a better understanding of the job. They are relieved they have survived the first half of the year.

Reflection Phase

This is the time teachers review their curriculum, management, and teaching strategies. It is a "what worked and what will I do different" stage. The end of the year is approaching, and they start thinking about next year. It is a time of self-analysis. (Moir, 1999)

Mentors: Supporters and Guides

Mentoring programs to induct and support new teachers, which became popular in the '80s, can be highly effective. "The assignment of a support teacher may well be the most powerful and cost-effective induction practice available to program developers" (Huling-Austin & Murphy, 1987, pp. 35-36).

The word "mentor" comes from the character Mentor, in Homer's *Odyssey*, who was chosen to educate and support Telemachus while his father was fighting in the Trojan War. The word now means a wise and trusted friend, and the role has expanded to include teacher, supporter, guide, protector, and sponsor.

Many studies have been made of the partnerships between mentors and novice teachers. They provide evidence of the positive impact these relationships have on new teachers' orientation to the school system, socialization to the school culture, and improved effectiveness in promoting student learning. "Mentor teachers have become known as occupational life savers known for offering technical, social, and emotional support" (Bey, 1995, p. 11).

Support by Design

Mentors support new teachers in many different ways. When designing or selecting a mentoring program for new teachers, let's think about it in terms of this analogy.

Suppose you are studying the reintroduction of wolves in the lower 48, and you want to learn more about it at the site of Yellowstone National Park. You make plans to visit the park and seek out a ranger when you arrive. You describe your interests, and the ranger asks you several questions: "Have you ever been here before?" "What specifically do you want to learn?" "How much time and money do you have to support your stay?" Your answers will help the ranger advise you of your options.

If you have never visited the park before, the first things you will need to know are: the park layout, including the location of food and facilities; the rules for being in the park; and the opening and closing times. What you want to learn about the wolves will affect the ranger's recommendations, including whether it would be wise to have a park service guide accompany you. If you want a guide, the experience will be different depending on whether you have an hour and want a quick walk around the perimeter of the habitat, or if you can stay longer. Perhaps you could become part of a small group that would spend four hours walking through the area of the park you want to see. If you said that you had several days to devote to your observations, you might arrange for a ranger who is very knowledgeable to join you each day and share her or his knowledge, assisting you while you make your observations and answering your questions along the way. Each level of interaction would be useful to you and, depending on your priorities and resources, you would make a decision about the course of action to pursue.

Designing a mentoring program for new teachers is similar to visiting the park. Your system may want mentors to orient new teachers to the school and provide information about routines and practices. Providing new teachers with this information is helpful. If mentors have additional time to interact with new teachers, they can discuss the curriculum and some methods of instruction they have found successful. If your system is able to free up classroom teachers for more time, or create full-time mentor positions, those mentors might do cognitive coaching on a regular basis throughout the school year, working side by side with new teachers as they become even better instructors. The extent and the depth of interactions between mentors and new teachers are determined by decisions about goals and resource allocation made when the program was created.

Let's look at some of the functions mentors may perform, depending on choices your system makes about time, personnel, and funding. Just as with your visit to Yellowstone and the support of the park rangers, there are different levels of guidance that mentors may provide for new teachers. Setting up a mentoring program is a complicated process that requires planning and commitment.

Four Ways Mentors Can Support New Teachers

Provide emotional support and encouragement

Many new teachers feel a significant degree of self-doubt as they encounter the challenges of teaching students with diverse learning and emotional needs. In fact, 15 percent of new teachers leave in their first year, and 15 percent leave in their second year (though the typical rate of turnover in the teaching profession is 6 percent), according to a study by Schlechty and Vance (1983, p. 476). While teachers leave for many reasons, those who have had mentors said repeatedly that it was the support and encouragement of the mentor, sometimes on a daily basis at the beginning of the year, which made the difference in their ability to see the possibility of themselves becoming competent and successful teachers (Huling-Austin & Murphy, 1987). Trust and rapport with new teachers is established by mentors in as many ways as there are new teachers, yet what is true for all is a positive presupposition of the new teacher's worth and good intentions. When mentors convey this mind-set, they are able to help new teachers believe they will be able to meet their teaching responsibilities, and put their energies toward learning more about their practice.

This may be particularly important when teachers who have been specifically recruited and hired because of their diversity enter a school system in which there are not many teachers who share their cultural identity. Teachers of color, as well as teachers of different ethnicities or religions, often face unique challenges if they are recruited into predominantly white school communities. "Differences in sex, race, ethnicity, socioeconomic background, or educational background can thwart the initial expectations of a mutually beneficial alliance and the unconscious identification process that frequently sets mentor relationships in motion. Self-awareness and a repertoire of interpersonal skills are prerequisites for overcoming these additional barriers" (Kram, 1985, p. 199).

Teachers in the minority are often called upon whenever a student who shares their cultural identity is having a problem. Colleagues often turn to them as if they were representatives of their race/ethnicity/religion, instead of as individuals who have their own experiences and perspectives. People of color or who are different in other visible ways are often scrutinized more than people in the majority, and as a result may feel significant pressure to "be perfect." In addition, if people of color live in the communities in which they have been recruited to work, they may feel even more isolated and separated from familiar aspects of their culture.

Doreen Ballard, a protégé in a recent study of mentoring, commented, "In order for someone, a female or someone of color to be successful, they have to have a good support system, a good mentor who is willing to take the time to mentor them, to listen to them and to guide them, give them advice and be there for them" (Gardiner, Enomoto, & Grogan, 2000, p. 176). Mentors of new teachers whose cultural identity is in the minority need to understand and acknowledge these additional factors and the possible impact on their partner's ability to deal with all the other issues faced by new teachers. Mentors are in a position to make even more of a difference in their partners' adjustment and acceptance if they provide support based on greater awareness of the issues (Crow & Matthews, 1997).

It is often considered optimal for people to be mentored by teachers sharing their minority status because they have had common experiences. There are also benefits to cross-cultural mentoring, as both teachers learn from each other and may gain additional insight from hearing each other reflect on their experiences (Kram, 1985).

Provide information about the daily workings of the school and the cultural norms of the school community

Experienced teachers show new teachers where the supplies are kept, familiarize them with the way things are done, and are available to answer questions. Formalizing what is probably happening spontaneously in schools is useful to new teachers. This is an important and necessary component of new teachers' entry.

Newcomers appreciate having buddies and can benefit from their knowledge of the school culture. Mentors can alert newcomers to things that they would not have found written anywhere and might only learn about after they had inadvertently gone against the norm. For example, suppose teachers in a school leave the school building shortly after the students are dismissed. There are many reasons why they might, including custodial hours, perceived safety of the neighborhood, or stated preference of the administration. Their not staying late might also be related to an unpublicized "work to rule" practice adopted by the teachers because of unresolved contractual issues. A new teacher who remained in that school after the other teachers had left could be treated with animosity, and she might not know why.

In another school, suppose teachers remain in school for several hours after the students leave, collaborating and socializing with each other. A new teacher might prefer to leave school and go for a walk after student dismissal, or care for an elderly relative before working long hours at home preparing for the next day. Yet in this situation, colleagues might think the new teacher isn't working hard because they don't see him working after school.

New teachers need to know the cultural norms before they can decide which ones they want to follow. Mentors can tell them "the way things are done here" in advance, or notice when there are misperceptions. Then, as buddies, they can help the new teacher sort through the misunderstandings.

And yet, as helpful as it is to have a buddy, new teachers need much more.

Promote cultural proficiency regarding students and their families

New teachers need assistance in another way when they are unfamiliar with the cultural diversity of their students and its impact on their learning. New teachers might misread or misinterpret student classroom behaviors and, in so doing, may not respond to their students in ways that promote achievement in school. Delpit states, "Teacher candidates are told that 'culturally different' children are mismatched to the school setting and therefore cannot be expected to achieve as well as White, middle class children. They are told that children of poverty are developmentally slower than other children" (1992, p. 245). Delpit cites numerous examples of teachers identifying the actions and words of students from different cultures as signals of a lack of ability rather than displays of cultural diversity. It is therefore crucial that mentors teach techniques to novice teachers that address these possible failures in communication and understanding. In addition, mentors are in a strong position to help change parts of school policies and/or practices that are unsatisfactory for student learning.

Cognitive coaching

When a mentor coaches a new teacher, significant growth is possible for both of them. Cognitive coaching, or peer coaching, is a powerful way for teachers at different stages in their careers to heighten each other's effectiveness. Through a process of pre-observation conferencing, nonjudgmental classroom observation, and post-observation conferencing, mentors may be very helpful to new teachers. Prompting self-reflection through the collection and sharing of data from classroom observations, as well as asking thoughtful questions that promote reflection, are the key strategies of successful cognitive coaching. Coaching by a mentor during a teacher's first year in the system may establish peer coaching as a norm of behavior that will serve the new and experienced teachers well after the completion of the induction program, in addition to helping new teachers learn more of their craft at an earlier point in their careers.

Some mentoring programs last through the new teacher's second, and sometimes third, year in the system. Cognitive coaching during these years may provide the most in-depth, continuous process for both teachers to examine their practices.

Professional Development for New Teachers

New teachers need more than orientation to the school system. They benefit from ongoing professional development in a number of aspects of their teaching responsibilities, including classroom management, curriculum standards and assessment, alternate ways to meet the needs of diverse student populations, promoting parent and community involvement, problem solving, conflict resolution, and time management.

New teachers benefit from meeting with each other regularly; they realize that they are not alone in their feelings of being overwhelmed, uncertain about their competence, and/or confused by some of their experiences. They are also able to share coping strategies, as well as things that have been successful in their classroom teaching.

Experienced teachers who are new to a school have somewhat different needs. They also need to be familiarized with the school's policies and practices, as well as the school culture. Yet they may not have the same needs for development in the additional topics previously mentioned. Instead, it may be useful for them to participate in one or more school or districtwide committees, along with teachers who have been in the district a number of years. In this way, they have a chance to get to know colleagues, their expertise is recognized, and they learn more in the process of working with colleagues on an important topic.

An induction program for new teachers that is part of a larger plan of professional development for all teachers in the school system has the potential for the most benefits. For example, if a school system uses the Dimensions of Learning to discuss curriculum and instruction, it would be ideal for new teachers also to learn something about the Dimensions during their induction. Their awareness of the Dimensions will enable new teachers to converse with other teachers in the system, using a common language and knowledge base.

> When colleagues in different stages of their careers are using the same language, and focusing on achieving the same student outcomes, there is a synergy in the school community that can be transformative.

Qualities of Good Mentors

Who will mentor the new teachers? One teacher, in describing her mentor, said, "No matter how much my little ship is tossed about, I know there's a good strong anchor" (Villani, 1999). Thinking about a mentor we had, or wished we had, often yields a list of admirable qualities. DeBolt (1989, p. 19) notes that mentors rated the following as the most helpful characteristics for their mentoring:

- Approachability
- Integrity
- Ability to listen
- Sincerity
- Willingness to spend time
- Enthusiasm
- Teaching competence
- Trustworthiness
- Receptivity
- Willingness to work hard
- Positive outlook
- Confidence
- Commitment to the profession
- Openness

- Experience in teaching
- Tactfulness
- Cooperativeness
- Flexibility

When mentors know how others mentor, they are often inclined to expand their repertoires (Villani, 1983).

Mentor Preparation

Mentors are best able to do their work when they explicitly learn about their role. Understanding about adult development, the needs of new teachers, and strategies that promote reflection and growth makes mentors more effective. The work mentors do varies depending on the level of knowledge, skills, and emotional development of their new-teacher partners. Training and continuing support are key factors in the success of mentoring programs. On the basis of data from mentor teachers' logs, Odell (1990) suggested that mentor teachers need training on the following:

1. The purposes of teacher induction programs
2. School district philosophy, needs, and priorities
3. District policies and operating procedures
4. Working with the adult learner; stages of teacher development
5. Concerns and needs of beginning teachers
6. Clinical supervision, classroom observation, and conferencing skills
7. Teacher reflection, and fostering self-esteem and self-reliance in the novice teacher (as cited in Huling-Austin, 1992, p. 176)

The Power of Mentoring

Most experienced teachers who are motivated to become mentors for altruistic reasons find that they "get as much as they give." One experienced teacher, in describing the benefits of mentoring a novice colleague wrote, "New ideas, viewpoint, rethinking my beliefs, fun, sense of being useful—sharing my own skills and knowledge—re-energizing" (Concord, MA Public Schools/Concord-Carlisle, MA High School Mentor Program Final Evaluation, 1994.)

Not only do teachers find that they learn more about their own teaching as they convey what they know to new teachers, they also find that peer coaching enables them to go deeper into their own practice.

There are also noteworthy benefits for other members of the school community. The entire school culture may be positively affected by mentoring programs for several reasons. Mentors are often energized when they teach other adults. Teachers find it rejuvenating to talk with colleagues who are interested in exploring with them the best practices in curriculum and instruction. Isolation, often one of the most difficult aspects of teaching, is usually reduced, if not eliminated, for teachers who participate in mentoring programs.

Aspiring teachers are becoming more aware of the benefits of mentoring programs. During interviews, they often ask what types of support are available. A comprehensive induction program can offer districts a competitive advantage as they recruit and seek to retain new teachers.

Other teachers who are not directly participating in the program are also affected by the enthusiasm and camaraderie of new teachers and their mentors. Since it takes more than one person to support a new teacher, experienced staff in the school may step up to share the responsibility. When this happens, many members of the school community are pursuing excellence through mutual support and reflection.

2

Beginning With New
Teachers and Continuing:
Program Design

You need to make decisions about the goals of the program you select or design, keeping in mind the needs of new teachers and the means to support them. Funding, the roles of supporters, and evaluation are important considerations as you move toward defining your program. These and other variables described in this chapter will help you consider the different models in Part 2.

Goals

What are your goals for the program? Do you need to satisfy a state mandate for mentoring as part of certification for new teachers? Do you want to orient and induct first-year teachers to your system, familiarizing them with the culture of your schools? Are you intent on welcoming first-year teachers to the profession, supporting some of them through the often-difficult transition from being a student and young adult to being the teacher "in charge," and supporting others who may have changed careers to teach? Will the program be part of a larger picture of professional development, designed for all teachers in the system, to address the diverse learning needs of students and heighten their achievement? Are you determined to find ways to retain the teachers you hire because you are concerned about the number of teachers who leave the profession in their first few years?

17

Huling-Austin (1989, p. 9) identified the following five goals of most induction programs:

1. Improve teacher performance
2. Increase retention of promising beginning teachers during the induction years
3. Promote the personal and professional well-being of beginning teachers
4. Satisfy mandated requirements
5. Transmit the culture of the system

Think about the visit to Yellowstone and the different plans made according to the purposes of the trip and the available resources. You need to clarify your priorities as you consider options for inducting your new faculty. Satisfying mandated requirements is a responsibility that must be addressed. Yet it is only the beginning. You need to think about your system's new teachers and what is essential for their success. Promoting their personal and professional well-being and transmitting the culture of your system are basic ingredients in any induction program.

> The biggest challenge you face in establishing or refining your program is how best to facilitate enhanced teacher performance, with the ultimate goal of heightening student achievement with the resources available to you.

The mentoring programs described take various approaches to improving teachers' effectiveness. Focusing solely on new teachers yields a different program from one that addresses professional development for all faculty. You need to be cognizant of the needs of teachers in different stages of their development as professional educators. Teachers certified after completing a degree in higher education will be prepared differently from new teachers who come to education from another career; experienced teachers who are new to your district will seek other qualities in your induction program. You must be mindful of all new faculty as you contemplate program design.

Funding

Funding is often the first consideration when envisioning a new program. You may be wondering if your district can afford a mentoring program. The question is rather

> Can you afford not to have an induction program?

The estimated costs of recruiting, hiring, and orienting a new teacher varies greatly, from $5,000 to $50,000, depending on the degree of professional development incorporated in estimating the cost of the induction process. Given the growing number of teachers we need to hire in the next ten years, we cannot afford to replace the 40 percent who may leave the profession. We have a fiscal responsibility, as well as educational and organizational ones, to keep the teachers we are hiring in the profession. Viewed this way, funding a program is a necessity, not a luxury.

It's important not to limit your thinking in the initial phases of investigation because of cost considerations. In addition to being a line item in the school system's annual budget, there are other ways to support your mentoring program. These include the following:

- Funding and/or grants from your state
- Grants from local education funds and/or parent-teacher organizations
- Funding from your local teachers' association
- Use of other professional development monies in your budget
- Personnel sharing or reassignment

It is very important to acknowledge and value mentors for their time and efforts. In addition to monetary stipends for mentors, there are other things school systems may do for mentors. These include the following:

- Recognition in the school system for becoming a mentor; status
- Compensatory time, for professional or personal use
- Support to attend professional development opportunities outside of the school system

- Released time from teaching to work with colleagues
- Common planning periods for mentors and new-teacher partners
- Reduced duties, such as supervision in study halls, the cafeteria, or at recess

Supporters

While mentors are the primary supporters of new teachers, there are others who are positioned to ease their entry into teaching. Administrators can make sure that new teachers aren't asked to face all the challenges of education during their first year. Coordination surely makes an impact on the success of the program. You have to make decisions about these crucial factors.

Mentors

In considering a mentoring program for your school system, you need to consider who will mentor, and whether they will do it in addition to their teaching responsibilities, as full-time work, or some combination of classroom teaching and mentoring. Inviting retired teachers to be mentors is an idea that is receiving increasing consideration. As more teachers are retiring, the number of new teachers may actually exceed the number of experienced teachers in a particular grade level or department.

There are benefits to having classroom teachers mentor new colleagues. Experienced teachers in the building are familiar with the issues classroom teachers address because they are facing them each day. Experienced classroom teachers have high credibility. They know the school culture and are in the best position to introduce new teachers to the people and protocols in their school. Their knowledge of curriculum, especially if they are assigned to mentor a new teacher in their grade or subject area, is current and includes many instructional strategies for helping students achieve the desired learning outcomes.

On the other hand, classroom teachers have many responsibilities to their students and families. It may be difficult for them to make time to mentor new colleagues when they already have so many other demands on them. Finding time to do peer coaching during the school day may be particularly difficult, especially if the school system cannot afford, or has a paucity of, substitute teachers to provide coverage. Using preparation periods for mentoring increases the amount of work that mentors need to do after school hours. It's a lot to ask of people, especially when these teachers are often the ones who are also on many of the school system committees because of their capabilities and commitment.

Teaching is a career with a relatively flat organizational structure, especially in elementary schools. Mentoring can be a much-needed way to support the developmental needs of experienced teachers. In other words, they can stretch professionally.

> Mentoring is often a powerful experience for master teachers who remain passionate about classroom teaching and are ready for an additional challenge.

Full-time mentors are able to devote themselves to new teachers, and don't have the conflicting demands of a class of their own. They can be trained in many aspects of mentoring, and have the time to provide support on instructional and curriculum issues. Full-time mentors can accommodate the new teacher's schedule more easily when they do observations and conferencing because they aren't concerned about coverage of their own students. Nor is there the additional expense of substitutes.

However, many full-time mentors often coach new teachers in several schools and may not be available for spontaneous questions and unanticipated events. Also, full-time mentors are not members of each specific school community, so their knowledge of school culture may be limited. Their credibility may be lower because they are not currently classroom teachers, especially if it has been many years since they were teaching in the classroom. For this reason, some school systems with full-time mentors require that the mentors return to the classroom after a specified number of years, often two or three, so that they maintain their identity as classroom teachers.

In all scenarios, it is likely that the skills of the support providers will be enhanced. Whether they remain in the classroom, return to the classroom after a period of time as a full-time mentor, or continue to be support providers, the experience of mentoring is consistently beneficial to veteran teachers.

Administrators

Principals can show their support of the mentoring program by describing it during the interview process, as well as reiterating it when welcoming new teachers. Arranging common planning time for mentors and their new teacher partners is a visible way for principals to demonstrate that new teacher induction is a priority. Sometimes principals align specialist schedules so that mentors are able to meet with their new-teacher partners during common preparation times. In addition, principals promote cognitive coaching as a value of the school, as well as the mentor program, when they arrange classroom coverage so mentors may observe and coach new teachers.

One of the conundrums of our profession is that we often assign new teachers the most challenging situations: a high percentage of students with diverse learning and emotional needs; the least desirable schedules; inadequate classrooms and materials; and the largest number of class preparations.

> Administrators must be vigilant about safeguarding new teachers from these especially difficult assignments during their first three years.

It is also important for administrators to consider the effect on new teachers of coaching sports or being advisors for extracurricular activities. It may be tempting to think of new teachers' talents and enthusiasm for these roles when recruiting. However, new teachers cannot enhance their teaching and grow in their first few years if they are dividing their attention between teaching in the classroom and after-school activities. Administrators may show their support of new teachers by encouraging them not to be involved in extracurricular activities during their first two years.

Coordinators/Steering Committee

Coordination of the mentor program is another important consideration when planning to implement or modify a program in your school system. The large number of things school educators are required to do make it difficult for them to focus on mentoring if it is not a specific job responsibility. When someone is the designated director or coordinator, things are more likely to operate smoothly, and the mentors and new teachers know there is someone shepherding the program. Any unexpected difficulties, as well as the day-to-day issues of teaching and mentoring, may be addressed more expeditiously because someone takes that specific responsibility.

A building administrator is usually not the best choice for overseeing the mentoring program because of issues of confidentiality. Principals are understandably interested in the induction of their new teachers. However, their direct involvement in the mentoring program may reduce the feelings of safety concerning evaluation that some new teachers experience.

Sometimes the assistant superintendent for curriculum and instruction coordinates the program. The responsibility of coordination may be assigned to another person in the system who has experience in the program. Creating a position solely for the direction of the program is optimal.

To E or Not to E

A key consideration in new teacher induction is evaluation. Will mentors be non-evaluative supporters, or will they make recommendations about new teachers' continued employment? Mentoring is usually viewed as a separate function from supervision and evaluation. Traditionally it has been considered a non-evaluative role, in which the new teacher presumably feels more comfortable confiding in a mentor about struggles and challenges. Many mentoring programs have been predicated on the separation of mentoring and evaluation.

Several states have formalized the induction program for new teachers and linked it to licensure. Connecticut, for example, requires that mentoring of new teachers be part of the certification process. When Connecticut's program was first developed, mentors were trained and assigned to support and evaluate new teachers; now the assessment function is done at the state level through a portfolio review process, and mentors support new teachers in portfolio development.

There are some mentoring programs in which peer evaluations are a significant factor in the continued employment of the new teachers. The Peer Assistance and Review (PAR) program in Toledo, Ohio, was the first such endeavor to gain nationwide attention, and others have been developed. These programs are agreements between the teachers' union and the school administration regarding peer involvement in the evaluation of new teachers and their induction. The PAR programs are noteworthy because they are contrary to the popular notion of mentoring. Advocates for this form of support believe that experienced teachers are the most qualified to provide support as well as gatekeep for the profession.

Confidentiality

Safety is a primary consideration for creating an environment conducive to learning. New teachers need to know whether their candidly shared concerns will be kept confidential, as they decide how much to share with their mentors. Trust is a key component in the relationship.

Many programs assure new teachers that mentors will not share anything about them with administrators. In peer assistance and review programs that have been negotiated by the union and the administration, new teachers know what aspects of their relationship with mentors are confidential, as well as that the mentor will make recommendations regarding their rehiring. Adam Urbanski, President of the Teachers' Union in Rochester, New York, stated, "The relationship is confidential, though the outcome is public."

Other teachers need to understand the nature of the mentoring relationship so that they may be supportive of new teachers. In a positive school climate, teachers form relationships with new colleagues and speak directly with them. Mentors should not discuss new teachers' performance, and should not listen to comments about their partners from other teachers.

> When new teachers know that the members of their
> school community are interested in promoting their
> growth and success, they are more likely to thrive.

Duration

Many mentoring programs span the first year of a new teacher's employment with the school system. The goal is to get the teacher off to a good start. Cognitive coaching may be a component of the program, with the hope that teachers will see the benefits and continue doing it after the program ends. Other school systems see the mentoring process as a two-years-or-longer endeavor, and plan for it as a part of the overall professional development of teachers in the district. You will want to think about the way in which you envision mentoring in your setting. Will it be designed for the entry of new teachers? Will it be part of a larger plan for professional development, going well beyond orientation and induction, and becoming a way to share common skill-sets and approaches to teaching?

Professional Development Throughout a Teaching Career

Many school systems are extending mentoring for periods longer than one year because new teachers need more than a year to learn what they need to know. Feiman-Nemser advocates for long-term support that goes beyond helping teachers feel comfortable in the school culture to addressing their developmental process of building confidence and heightening competence (Feiman-Nemser, 1994). The mentor's role is to promote new teachers' reflection on their practice; in so doing, mentors often reflect on their own practice as well.

Reiman and Thies-Sprinthall have studied ways to promote mentors' skills. They have found that the combination of helping someone else learn, which they call role-taking, and reflection yield the greatest learning for mentor trainees. Reflection could take the form of journaling, sequenced readings, and discussions of role-taking experiences. They found that a balance between the role-taking and the reflection is important, and it works best when there is guided reflection once a week (Reiman, 1998).

In an induction program that emphasizes long-term support and focuses on instructional practice through cognitive coaching, the benefits of role-taking and reflection to new teachers and veteran teachers are likely to be significant.

Mentoring and the Stages of Teaching

The stages of teaching are useful to consider, as you plan or revise your mentoring program for new teachers, because they suggest ways you can be addressing some of the developmental needs of the mentors as well.

Continuum of Mentorships to Support Phases of Teacher Change

Recruitment: *Prospective teachers*
Provides pre-career counseling and information for individuals who have an interest in the teaching

Pre-certification preparation: *Student teachers*
Supervises and guides teacher candidates in making the transition between theory and practice

Apprenticeship: *Intern teachers*
Advises new initiates about the fundamental teaching practices and skills needed to be successful in the classroom

Developmental growth: Beginning teachers
Consults and assists beginning teachers with their personal and professional concerns, needs, and challenges

Expansionary growth: Career teachers
Encourages career-committed teachers to analyze and refine existing teaching practices, as well as incorporate new teaching practices

Meritorious achievement: *Master teachers*
Aids efforts to help exemplary teachers promote the technical knowledge and research on teaching (Bey, 1995, p. 16)

Your new teachers are in the stages of apprenticeship and developmental growth, and your mentors are in the stages of expansionary growth and meritorious achievement. Bey proposes a continuum of mentorships designed to develop, integrate, and support phases of teacher change, and she suggests that mentoring partnerships are developmental episodes throughout the stages of life.

Some portray mentoring as a role of activism, by which experienced teachers can actually move their partners and others to change parts of the system that are not functional. "As proactive change agents, mentors function as the sponsors of actions to reform education. They empower others to rethink obsolete routines and be accountable for continued improvement" (Fullan, 1993, as cited in Bey, 1995, p. 15).

> Mentoring clearly has the potential to be a catalyst in school improvement as well as professional development.

Collaboration: Inside and Outside of School

School systems that are near a college or university have opportunities for coordinating pre-service and/or induction of new teachers with college faculty. There are a multitude of ways that faculty in institutions of higher education may supplement and complement the induction and professional development of new teachers. Sometimes college faculty members support new teachers individually in their schools, and other times they sponsor seminars or topical sessions for new teachers.

Collaboratives, or consortia, are ways that educational institutions are able to pool their talents and resources for the induction of new teachers, as well as provide many other aspects of professional development. Some school systems team up to train mentors and new teachers. Others hold jointly sponsored conferences or workshops that would not be individually affordable for any of the districts. Telecommunication is another model that is being explored, especially in places where distance and population density are factors that require special consideration.

Collaborations with the teachers' association, local institutions of higher education, and educational networks expand the ways that school systems can support their new, as well as their veteran, teachers. Some bridges among these groups are already established in school systems, and others can be created with the common goal of inducting and retaining new teachers.

The support of the teachers' association, the school committee, and the central office administration are invaluable contributors to the success, if not existence, of any program. When all members of the school community are united in their commitment to the new teachers, all the energy is moving in the same direction. The message is welcoming to the new teachers and clear to everyone: We are dedicated to supporting our new teachers, and are devoting some of our resources to their success.

Part 2

Models of Mentoring/
Induction of New Teachers

The following chapters describe models of mentoring that represent different approaches to the induction of new teachers. These programs were selected because they give you a sense of the range of possibilities. They exemplify ways that educational institutions at the local and state level have supported new teachers and, in the process, have benefited veteran faculty as well.

The models are grouped by funding sources, for the most part. Chapter 3 includes districts that mainly support their mentoring programs through local budgets. Chapter 5 includes programs that are largely supported by state funds. Connecticut, for example, has articulated induction requirements, though the way some of them are addressed is at the local level. Chapters 6 and 7 describe programs that are funded by large grants or in ways that have creatively dealt with the need for programs without a large infusion of money from state or local sources. Chapter 4 highlights two programs that were developed and implemented through extensive collaborations with the teachers' unions. These programs are not grouped by funding sources, yet are examples of ways that negotiations have addressed financial and other contractual issues in new ways.

Each model is presented in the same format. Two tables summarize the demographics and key features of each program. Descriptions of the models are presented in a question-and-answer format, which facilitates comparison and may help you select the ones that have the greatest relevance for your school/district/state. Perhaps you will find one that you want to replicate, or you may think that one or two of them have promise for your system, with some customization for your specific situations.

3

Programs Funded by the School System/District/Region

Aurora Public Schools Induction Process
Aurora, Colorado

Dover-Sherborn Public Schools Teacher Leaders Program
Dover, Massachusetts

Glendale Union High School District
Glendale, Arizona

Newport News Public Schools Instructional Mentoring Program
Newport News, Virginia

Francis Howell School District Mentoring Program
Saint Charles, Missouri

Saint Paul Public Schools Learning Circles/Mentor Program for New Teachers
Saint Paul, Minnesota

AURORA PUBLIC SCHOOLS INDUCTION PROCESS
AURORA, COLORADO

Kay Shaw, Director of Staff Development
Administration Building, 1085 Peoria Street
Aurora, Colorado 80011
303-344-8060, x28053
kays@admin.aps.k12.co.us
As of July 9, 2001

DEMOGRAPHICS

The following figures are for the 2000-2001 school year.

Grade Levels	K-12 and post-secondary	Urban/Suburban/Rural	Urban
Student Population	28,313	Ethnic Makeup* African American Asian American Caucasian Hispanic Native American	25% 4% 42% 28% 1%
Teacher Population	1,839	% New Teachers	14%
		Per Pupil Expenditure	$4,947

* The statistics available from the district delineated the ethnic makeup as shown.
There was no information about students of more than one racial heritage.

The following information is quoted from written materials printed by the Aurora Public Schools, and telephone conversations and e-mail correspondence with Kay Shaw, Director of Staff Development.

History

The Aurora Public Schools established a task force of teachers and administrators with the primary charge of developing and monitoring an induction program for educators in compliance with the new Educator Licensure Act that was passed by the Colorado Legislature in 1991.

MENTOR PROGRAM

Unique Feature of Program	Continuum of skills correlated with each state standard; District resource teachers support mentors	Mentoring Is/ Is Not Mandated for Certification/ Licensing	Is mandated; Induction is mandated, and mentoring is a part of induction
Cognitive Coaching Is/ Is Not a Component	Is a component	Mentors Do/Do Not Evaluate the New Teachers With Whom They Work	Do not evaluate
Cost of Program	$95,500	Funding	District and grants
Mentors Are Full-Time/ Part-Time Teachers	Mentors: Full-time; District resource teachers: Full-time	Mentor Renumeration	Mentor: Varies $250-600; District resource teacher: Varies $750-2,200
Program in Existence	6 years	Duration of Program for New Teachers	1 year
Higher Education Affiliation	None	Program Coordinator	Kay Shaw

State Mandates

Is mentoring mandated for new teachers?

The Educators Licensure Act (HB 91–1005) was passed in 1991. It requires all school districts to implement an induction program for newly hired teachers, principals, and administrators holding provisional licenses. July 1, 1999 was the final date to have induction programs fully in place.

Is mentoring part of certification or licensure?

Mentoring is part of the induction process. Participating in an induction program is required for licensure.

Is funding provided to support the mandate?

No, the mandate to implement an induction program is not supported by funding.

Goals

1. Enhance the instructional skills of the individual
2. Enhance the leadership skills of the individual
3. Provide an understanding of the working culture of the Aurora Public Schools
4. Establish professional expectations
5. Provide a collaborative support network for new teachers, principals, and administrators
6. Increase the retention rates of high quality staff

Program Design

What are the components and recommended schedule of the program?

The induction program occurs from the time an individual enters the school district and continues throughout the first year (up to three years) of employment. The plan identifies tasks that occur before the first day of class, within the first two weeks of school, between the third and sixth week of school, and from the sixth to the eighteenth week of school. An integral part of the induction plan is the mentor program.

District resource teachers coordinate induction teams, each consisting of a protégé, his or her immediate supervisor (i.e., the building principal or designee who is responsible for the formal evaluation of the teacher) and a district-trained mentor. Mentors are designated at different levels (1–4) based on the amount of work they do with the new teachers.

The district staff development department equips new hires to build upon their instructional skills, classroom management strategies, professional expectations, and to understand the working culture of the Aurora Public Schools. Newly hired professionals are provided opportunities to learn district policies and perspectives in collaborative, supportive networks.

There is a three-day orientation for new teachers before school begins. At that time new teachers also meet their mentors.

Mentors are trained for two days before school begins, as well as at other times during the year.

Professional development experiences for teachers and special service-providers address:

1. Knowledge of content and learning
2. Variety of assessment approaches to improve learning
3. Understanding of democratic ideas
4. Appreciation and skills to work with the diversity of our population
5. Skills to communicate with students, parents, and colleagues in a professional manner

Are there any programs that complement the mentor program?

All new faculty are required to take a course, Teaching and Assessing the Content Standards. Also, additional days of training in other areas are offered; teachers who elect to take them have the option of financial reimbursement or credit on the salary scale.

Professional development efforts are conducted with attention to personal needs, comfort levels, and positive learning environments. Leadership skills are enhanced through invitations to participate in committee work, shared decision making, and district implementation of performance-based education.

Who designed the mentor program?

A districtwide study group, established through the staff development department:

1. Researched current induction programs in schools and in businesses
2. Identified the desired outcomes of those programs
3. Identified the elements that are highly successful in various induction programs
4. Identified the key service pieces
5. Determined the appropriate order/sequence of activities
6. Determined the roles and responsibilities of staff involved in such programs

As a result of this study group, the document "Continuum of Skills/Abilities for Professional Development," as well as timelines and optional methods of delivery, were created. The group worked within established parameters, but beyond the current paradigms of new employee training. They explored the wide variety of individual needs of new hires and recommended best practices to meet those needs. The new employees were surveyed to determine the benefit of the training and the merit of the mentor program in order to improve the existing plan. The study group spent the fall of 1994 studying the program and during the spring of 1995 made recommendations as per the requirements of Standards 13.00 and 14.00 of the Rules for Licensure.

The Task Force approved the hiring of district resource teachers. This position was started in the fall of 1995. District resource teachers (DRTs) are identified each spring and help with program implementation, program evaluation, and monitoring. The addition of the DRT positions assures greater program accountability and facilitates ongoing program development.

Program Administration

Who coordinates the mentor program?

Kay Shaw, Director of Staff Development, coordinates the program.

How is information communicated to shareholders?

The mentor program has a newsletter that is published five to seven times a year. Mentors are involved in two meetings for mentors and three formal induction meetings for mentors and protégés.

Who coordinates the integration of the mentor program with other professional development opportunities/requirements in the school/ district?

As Director of Staff Development, Kay is in an excellent position to coordinate the integration of the induction program with the other professional development opportunities and requirements in the school district.

Participants

Who is served?

The induction program is designed for all individuals who join the school district. These people are referred to as protégés in the mentor program.

Teachers changing grade level or subject area and those returning to the profession are assigned buddies, and may attend the new teacher class.

Is participation of new teachers voluntary or mandatory?

Participation in the program is mandatory.

Who provides the mentoring/induction?

Classroom teachers, with the support of district resource teachers, provide the mentoring.

What are the criteria for being a mentor/district resource teacher?

The qualifications for mentors are:

1. A minimum of five years teaching experience in the Aurora Public Schools (APS) is recommended
2. Expertise as demonstrated in meeting or exceeding APS performance standards
3. Evidence of participation in district mentor training
4. Experience with buddying, mentoring, coaching, peer observation, etc.
5. Evidence of continuous personal and professional development
6. Current certification or professional license
7. Recommendation from principal/administrators

The qualifications required of district resource teachers are:

1. Master's degree or higher
2. Demonstrated expertise as teacher, by meeting or exceeding the APS performance standards
3. Experience with adult education, training, professional development, etc.
4. Experience with mentoring, coaching, peer observation, etc.
5. Understanding of HB 1005

What are the job responsibilities of the mentor/district resource teacher?
The mentor's job responsibilities are to:

1. Fulfill requirement as stated in the "Professional Development Support Plan"
2. Meet frequently with the protégé. Have regularly scheduled meetings to review the "Timeline for New Teachers' Activities"
3. Plan with the protégé, observe the protégé, and provide feedback
4. Serve as a role model in all aspects of the profession
5. Support the protégé, provide perspective when needed
6. Guide the protégé to familiarity with district/building procedures, programs and culture
7. Have a sincere commitment to the mentoring program and a willingness to invest time and effort to support it
8. Maintain confidentiality with the protégé
9. Assist in the development of personal goals for the protégé, along with the induction team
10. Be part of the induction team for the protégé, and participate in three meetings to review progress

Mentors work with new teachers and buddies work with newly hired teachers who have a certificate or a professional license.

The district resource teacher's responsibilities are to:

1. Select, train, and provide continued support for district mentors
2. Design and deliver induction training
3. Coordinate the matching of protégés with mentors
4. Coordinate meetings with protégés and mentors
5. Communicate with necessary parties
6. Provide resources, information, and support to principals, mentors, and protégés
7. Coordinate, design, and deliver staff development for protégés and mentors
8. Ensure induction teams are providing the necessary support for protégés
9. Ensure the district's compliance with State Board of Education Implementation Guidelines for HB 1005

Is peer observation and coaching a requirement of mentors?

Reflection training or cognitive coaching are recommended.

Do mentors/district resource teachers have full-time classroom teaching responsibilities?

Mentors, buddies, and district resource teachers have full-time teaching responsibilities.

How are mentors available to participate in the program?

Each mentor-protégé team is allowed two days of released time to observe, give feedback and/or go on visitations. Protégés determine the type of support they need.

How are mentors/district resource teachers selected?

Building principals select mentors.

District resource teachers are selected through an interview process that also includes assessment of writing skills and reflection skills.

Are mentors/district resource teachers paid?

Mentors elect to receive in-service credit or a stipend for the time spent. Such credit ranges from 0.5 credit hours to 2.0 credit hours in accordance with the Colorado Department of Education guidelines for course credit. Stipends range from $250 to $600 based on the level of mentor involvement.

How are matches made between mentors and new teachers? How are the matches made with district resource teachers?

Building principals match the mentors and the new teachers. They consider the grade level and subject area of the teacher. District resource teachers are assigned by locations to minimize the time they are traveling. They and the building principals have the option to decide whether the district resource teacher works another year in the building. District resource teachers work with all the mentors in the school.

Are mentors trained?

Yes. The course content for mentors includes training about:

1. The school and district culture
2. Adult learning theory
3. The change model (CBAM)

4. Research on beginning teacher needs and stages of the teaching career
5. The mentor's job description, including role and tasks
6. Mentor assessment and checklists
7. Calendars for guidance
8. The mentor-protégé relationship, including critical attributes of the mentoring relationship
9. Successful mentoring pairs and assessment of those relationships
10. Development of personal/professional goals

Buddies may participate in mentor training and mentor activities with other experienced staff to ensure that they are prepared to serve as mentors when needed

Who supervises mentors?

Kay supervises the mentors.

What supports are available for mentors?

Is there professional development for the mentors/district resource teachers?

Level 3 and 4 mentors are trained in cognitive coaching, as are district resource teachers. Level 3 and 4 mentors are the ones who spend a greater amount of time working with their protégés, as determined by mutual agreement.

Who provides it?

District resource teachers provide the training.

What resources are available for mentors?

There are district resource teachers who work with mentors to support new teachers. The DRTs each work with ten teams consisting of a protégé, mentor, and administrator. These teams meet three times a year to chart the progress of the protégé, and to support her or his growth.

This year a teacher on special assignment was selected to assist the mentor program. Other district personnel, including the curriculum coordinator, are available for additional support.

Do mentors evaluate new teachers?

No, mentors do not evaluate new teachers. Building principals evaluate each provisionally licensed teacher.

Is the mentor/new teacher relationship confidential?

Yes, the relationship between the mentor and the protégé is confidential.

What resources are required for the program?

1. Mentor training $8,500
2. New teacher orientation $5,000
3. Substitutes $5,000
4. Materials $ 2,000
5. Stipends for mentors and
   district resource teachers $75,000

Funding

What are the funding sources?

The district and some grant money fund the program.

Who requests the funding?

Kay requests the funding through the staff development department.

Evaluation of the Program

How is the program evaluated?

The protégé assesses the induction program, with the mentor's assistance. The process is ongoing and continues throughout the school year. Surveys are conducted, emphasizing evaluation of the training for personal needs, instructional needs, professional considerations, the climate and culture of the district, and information regarding district policy. Evaluation takes place near the end of the school year. The mentor training is evaluated within the mentor training sessions.

Who sees the results?

Kay, the mentors, and the district resource teachers see the results of the surveys.

Recruitment, Hiring, and Retention of New Staff

How many new teachers are recruited and hired?

250 teachers were hired in the 2000–2001 school year.

Is there any data that correlates the mentoring program with the retention of new teachers?

No.

What are the indicators of program success?

Respondents to the survey noted that the mentors, district resource teachers, other support personnel, and administrators were most helpful to new teachers' adjustment. They also cited the courses and the structure of the program as positive supports.

Dover-Sherborn Public Schools Teacher Leaders Program Dover, Massachusetts

Judith C. Klein, Teacher Leader
91 Elm Road
Newton, Massachusetts 02460
617-964-8897
weezer@world.std.com
As of July 9, 2001

Martin E. Moran, Teacher Leader
44 Oregon Road
Southborough, Massachusetts 01772
508-485-4696
moranm@doversherborn.org
As of July 9, 2001

The following information was obtained from telephone conversations and e-mail correspondence with Martin Moran and Kathy Dunne. Several quotations are taken from materials prepared by the Dover-Sherborn teacher leaders for use in the district and in their presentation at the National Staff Development Council's Annual Conference in Atlanta in 2000.

DEMOGRAPHICS

The following figures are for the 2000-2001 school year.

Grade Levels	K-12	Urban/Suburban/Rural	Suburban
Student Population	1,982	Ethnic Makeup* African American Asian American Caucasian Other	 2% 2% 95% 1%
Teacher Population	193	% New Teachers	16.5%
		Per Pupil Expenditure	$7,537

* The statistics available from the district delineated the ethnic makeup as shown.
  There was no information about students of more than one racial heritage.

MENTOR PROGRAM

Unique Feature of Program	Teacher leaders coordinate the program and do most of the training	Mentoring Is/ Is Not Mandated for Certification/ Licensing	Is not mandated
Cognitive Coaching Is/ Is Not a Component	Is a component	Mentors Do/Do Not Evaluate the New Teachers With Whom They Work	Do not evaluate
Cost of Program	$38,500	Funding	State grant, local education fund
Mentors Are Full-Time/ Part-Time Teachers	Full-time	Mentor Remuneration	Mentor: $750; Teacher leader: $1,000
Program in Existence	3 years	Duration of Program for New Teachers	1 year
Higher Education Affiliation	None	Program Coordinators	Scott Kellett, Judy Klein, Martin Moran, Barbara Pack, and Greg Tucker

History

John Moore, the middle school principal, had been matching new teachers with veteran staff in an informal way to promote the integration of the new staff into the school community. He wanted to formalize this matching process by creating a mentor program for new staff, to facilitate their success and promote their development as teachers. After a presentation to the administrative council about his concept, colleagues created mentor programs in their schools.

State Mandates

Is mentoring mandated for new teachers?

Yes.

Is mentoring part of certification or licensure?
No.

Is funding provided to support the mandate?
No.

Goals

The regional school district is faced with the challenge of replacing experienced staff members with those who are less experienced. The quality and excellence of the school system must be maintained during the transition. To facilitate this goal the school system should utilize the expertise of the experienced veteran staff.

The two major goals of the program are to attract and retain quality professionals and to improve the quality of instruction. The establishment of the program has the potential to raise the regard of the profession in the community and provide the opportunity for improved collegiality and morale. It also affords the opportunity for renewal for the veteran staff.

Program Design

The design of the program is one-to-one mentoring of new teachers and other professional development for them as well. In the course of mentoring, mentors also participate in professional development and grow.

What are the components and recommended schedule of the program?
The components of the program are:

1. Mentor training: End of August
2. Meetings of pairs, daily and then weekly: Throughout the school year
3. Afterschool workshops: Five times a year
4. Peer observations and cognitive coaching: Three times a year, optimally

The program officially begins when the mentors are chosen in the spring, and trained at the end of August. Just before school starts, the new teachers are told who their mentors will be for the school year.

The program technically ends at the close of school in June. However, many mentors are chosen as mentors for the following year, so their participation is cyclical. The teacher leaders work on design and plans for implementation of the program for the next year, so their participation is ongoing throughout the years.

Are there any programs that complement the mentor program?

In addition to the mentor, a support team is developed in each school to assist all the new teachers. The support team could include: the principal or headmaster, the assistant headmaster, a teacher leader, a department head, or other appropriate staff members.

Faculty who are not mentors support their new colleagues by welcoming them into their classrooms for observations and assisting when appropriate. Martin Moran videotapes colleagues, with their permission, whose teaching demonstrates different ways to approach some of the issues and questions raised by new teachers. The teacher leaders use the tapes at the afterschool meetings with the new teachers. Transitions and how to begin a lesson are two subjects that were videotaped.

Who designed the mentor program?

Kathy Dunne, an educational consultant with Learning Innovations at WestEd, was hired by John Moore to help him design and implement the initial mentor training. The following year, she worked with a select group of teacher leaders to: enhance their capacity to facilitate the mentor training; prepare them to serve as classroom coaches to support mentors as they deepen their coaching skills of working with new teachers; design and facilitate afterschool workshops for new faculty.

The teacher leaders planned the program for the upcoming year and put the dates for the trainings and workshops on the school calendars. They also designed and facilitated the afterschool workshops and arranged the substitutes' schedules.

Program Administration

Who coordinates the mentor program?

Teacher leaders are the linchpin in the operation of the mentor program. They are responsible for meeting with the other teacher leaders to coordinate the mentor program for the entire system. On the other hand, they work in conjunction with their building administrator(s) in coordinating the mentor program for their building. Their responsibilities include: overseeing the day-to-day operation of the program, initial training of mentors, holding afternoon workshops and organizing observation days for mentors and new teachers. If there are extra slots in the substitute's schedule, other teachers are welcome to use the time for peer coaching. The teacher leaders typically do not mentor new teachers; they coach the mentors. On rare occasions when needed, a teacher leader may mentor a new teacher.

How is information communicated to shareholders?

All members of the school community have been familiarized with the program. When it was first created, it was introduced to all adult shareholders.

Efforts are made by the teacher leaders and administrators to assure that everyone is aware of the mentor program and is familiar with its workings and the benefits it accrues. The teacher leaders, mentors, and new teachers are the most directly involved in such communication, and the administrators also discuss the program with faculty, school board members, and parents.

In addition, the teacher leaders have presented their program at different workshops and conferences, including the National Staff Development Council's (NSDC) annual conference in Atlanta in 2000. They have familiarized other educators with the mentor program they created and implement, and help them think about what they might want to do in their own districts.

Who coordinates the integration of the mentor program with other professional development opportunities/requirements in the school/ district?

The teacher leaders speak with the administrators periodically. The superintendent has said that the mentor program is the cornerstone of professional development in the district. A new professional development committee has been formed and discussions are under way to coordinate its efforts and those of the mentor program.

Participants

Who is served?

The program is designed for teachers who are new to the school system, either as novices or as educators joining from another school system.

Is participation of new teachers voluntary or mandatory?

The mentor program is discussed during the interviewing and hiring process, and it is seen as a benefit of employment. Participation in the program is expected of all new staff.

Who provides the mentoring/induction?

Mentors who are teaching colleagues are in a strong position to offer support and promote reflection without the presence of issues of evaluation and concerns about continued employment. Teachers are best able to support their colleagues in a nonjudgmental and non-threatening way.

What are the criteria for being a mentor?

1. Five years teaching experience, with at least two in the district
2. Demonstrated excellence in teaching
3. Demonstrated leadership in the school community
4. Strong communication skills

What are the job responsibilities of the mentors/teacher leaders?

Mentors are selected in the spring and trained in the summer. Each new teacher is assigned a mentor, with whom she or he meets very frequently in the beginning of the year and approximately weekly thereafter. Optimally, the mentors do cognitive coaching with their new teacher partners three times during the year. Substitutes are provided for the new teachers and mentors to observe each other teaching and to do the cognitive coaching. The teacher leaders, who coordinate the program, arrange the schedule for the substitutes.

There are also five afterschool meetings for the new teachers and their mentors, which are planned and led by the teacher leaders. These meetings last approximately one hour.

Is peer observation and coaching a requirement of mentors?

Yes. Ideally it is done at least three times during the school year.

Do mentors have full-time classroom teaching responsibilities?

Yes, mentors have full-time teaching responsibilities.

How are mentors available to participate in the program?

Training for mentors is offered at the end of August, before school begins.

Substitutes are hired and scheduled by teacher leaders to provide new teachers and their mentors the opportunity to do peer observations and cognitive coaching. There are workshops scheduled monthly after school.

Each teacher leader is relieved of one non-teaching duty per week to have time to orchestrate the program throughout the school year. Optimally they have a shared planning period each week with the other teacher leader in their building. The afterschool workshops and weekly meetings of pairs are done during teachers' preparation periods, lunch times, and before or after school hours.

How are mentors/teacher leaders selected?

Teachers volunteer to be mentors, sometimes at the request of building administrators. They are chosen by the building principal, often in consultation with teacher leaders, in accordance with the set of established criteria.

The teacher leaders are chosen by the building principals. These leaders are deemed effective teachers by the principals and the new teachers with whom they work, and have a background in cognitive coaching or *The Skillful Teacher*. It is presumed that other teachers will assume these roles in the future so that the program will be self-sustaining.

Are mentors/teacher leaders paid?

Yes, mentors are paid $750 a year, and teacher leaders are paid $1,000 a year.

How are matches made between mentors and new teachers?

The building administrators match the new teachers and mentors, often speaking with the teacher leaders about their ideas for matches. The grade level or subject area of the new teachers also influences the decisions for optimal partnerships.

Are mentors trained?

Yes, mentors are trained for two days in the summer, before school begins.

Who supervises mentors?

The teacher leaders supervise the mentors.

What supports are available for mentors?

Is there professional development for the mentors/teacher leaders?

There are five afterschool meetings of the new teachers and the mentors. The teacher leaders plan and implement these meetings. Prior to each meeting, Martin videotapes experienced teachers who are not part of the mentoring program, and these video clips are used during the afterschool meetings to exemplify topics being discussed. The involvement of other teachers has greatly affected the school culture.

The teacher leaders meet six times a year with Kathy Dunne. They discuss the program and ways to make it even stronger. In addition, some of the teacher leaders were part of a state-sponsored summer institute on mentoring. They worked with other school systems during the summer and occasionally during the school year to consult about teacher leadership and mentoring. In working with other consultants at these events, the teacher leaders learned more about presenting and consulting with groups of adults.

Who provides it?

The teacher leaders provide the professional development for the mentors, and coach them throughout the school year. Kathy Dunne works with the teacher leaders. The teacher leaders also work with other consultants when they participate in summer institutes on mentoring and induction programs for new teachers.

What resources are available for mentors/teacher leaders?

Mentors and teacher leaders have access to professional libraries and the audiovisual equipment they need for the program.

Do mentors evaluate new teachers?

No, mentors are involved in a nonjudgmental relationship with their colleagues.

Is the mentor/new teacher relationship confidential?

Yes, the relationship is completely confidential.

What are the resources required for the program?

1. Mentor handbook; new
   teacher handbook; supplies

for the mentor training and
afterschool workshops;
videotapes $1,000
2. Consultant time for the
   principal/teacher leaders $6,000
3. Stipends for mentors at
   $750 per person $22,500
4. Stipends for teacher leaders
   at $1000 per person $6,000
5. Substitutes for observations
   and planning meetings $3,000

Funding

What are the funding sources?

Initially John approached the local education foundation for money
to develop a mentor program, and was awarded $3,000. After his ini-
tial work with Kathy Dunne, he wrote a Goals 2000 grant, which was
awarded by the Massachusetts Department of Education, for
approximately $20,000. Both the Dover-Sherborn Education Founda-
tion and the Massachusetts Department of Education Goals 2000
Grant have funded additional proposals in the second and third
years of the program.

Who requests the funding?

John, and later the teacher leaders, request the funding.

Evaluation

How is the program evaluated?

The teacher leaders gather feedback from the new teachers and their
mentors in informal focus groups at the end of the school year. Based
on some of this feedback, the teacher leaders determine what the new
teachers are most interested in learning during the afterschool workshops. They use this feedback to inform and influence their design of
the program for the following year.

Who sees the results?

The mentor teacher leaders, John, and Kathy see the information gathered.

Recruitment, Hiring, and Retention of New Staff

How many new teachers are recruited and hired?

30 new teachers were hired in the 2000–2001 school year.

Is there any data that correlates the mentoring program with the retention of new teachers?

No.

What are program indicators of success?

The culture of the school system has dramatically changed in the last four years. Teachers are in and out of each other's classrooms. They welcome the new teachers and encourage them to sit in on their classrooms. The camaraderie among the mentors has also benefited the entire faculty of the school.

When the teacher leaders arrange the schedule of substitutes to cover new teachers and their mentors for observations and cognitive coaching, sometimes there are extra times that are not needed. Classroom teachers have requested the substitute so that they might do peer observations with other staff. This has been a significant change in school culture.

GLENDALE UNION HIGH SCHOOL DISTRICT
GLENDALE, ARIZONA

Vernon Jacobs, Associate Superintendent
7650 North 43rd Avenue
Glendale, Arizona 85301
623-435-6000
Fax: 623-435-6078
As of July 9, 2001

DEMOGRAPHICS

The following figures are for the 2000-2001 school year.

Grade Levels	9-12	Urban/Suburban/Rural	Suburban
Student Population	13,683	Ethnic Makeup* African American Asian American Caucasian Hispanic Native American	3.4% 5.6% 63.7% 25.0% 2.3%
Teacher Population	729	% New Teachers	14%
		Per Pupil Expenditure	$5,391

* The statistics available from the district delineated the ethnic makeup as shown.
There was no information about students of more than one racial heritage.

The following information was obtained from telephone conversations and e-mail correspondence with Vernon Jacobs, as well as printed materials from the program.

History

The Glendale Union High School District (GUHSD) had staff developers work with new teachers. When money got tight those positions were eliminated. Since the district had a strong commitment to the professional development of teachers, a collaborative effort by the administration and union developed a system to promote teacher excellence.

MENTOR PROGRAM

Unique Feature of Program	This is a 3-year program of support for new teachers in this high school regional district	Mentoring Is/ Is Not Mandated for Certification/ Licensing	Is not mandated
Cognitive Coaching Is/ Is Not a Component	Is a component	Mentors Do/Do Not Evaluate the New Teachers With Whom They Work	Do not evaluate
Cost of Program	$575,575/year	Funding	District
Mentors Are Full-Time/ Part-Time Teachers	Mentors teach 2 classes/day and mentor the remainder	Mentor Remuneration	Mentors are paid a teaching salary
Program in Existence	5 years	Duration of Program for New Teachers	3 years
Higher Education Affiliation	Arizona State University–West	Program Coordinator	Vernon Jacobs

It was decided that there would be mentors who taught two classes a day and then were released from teaching the other three periods a day for the purpose of supporting new teachers in their building. It was felt that having the mentors continue to teach would strengthen their identification with classroom teachers. Since the mentors were still classroom teachers the union would support their positions.

State Mandates

Is mentoring mandated for new teachers?
No.

Is mentoring part of certification or licensure?
No.

Is funding provided to support the mandate?

No.

Goals

- Accelerate good teacher decision making in the classroom.
- Retain quality first-, second-, and third-year teachers for a life-long career in the GUHSD.
- Provide support and improvement in instructional skills

Program Design

What are the components and recommended schedule of the program?

New teachers are mentored for 3 years by experienced teachers in the district. There is one mentor per school, and there are nine high schools in the regional district. The mentors work with all new teachers in their building during their first three years of employment in the GUHSD.

The new teachers come to work two weeks before the rest of the teachers, who return one week before the students. During the first two weeks the new teachers work with their mentors to prepare their classrooms. Preparation includes instructional training based on Madeline Hunter's Essential Elements of Instruction (EEI), classroom management based on Harry Wong's ideas, and discipline instruction by Fred Jones. They confer with a building team colleague, who shares lessons for the first nine weeks of school. The new teachers are paid to participate in these ten days of training.

Are there any programs that complement the mentor program?

District curriculum coordinators complement the mentor program by providing content workshops.

Who designed the mentor program?

Vernon Jacobs, Associate Superintendent of Curriculum and Instruction, and Norman Smalley, District Staff Developer, in collaboration with the union, developed the mentor program.

Program Administration

Who coordinates the mentor program?

Vernon Jacobs, the associate superintendent, coordinates the program.

How is information communicated to shareholders?

Vernon Jacobs communicates with the members of the school communities.

Who coordinates the integration of the mentor program with other professional development opportunities/requirements in the school/ district?

Vernon Jacobs coordinates this program with other professional development opportunities, as part of his role as associate superintendent.

Participants

Who is served?

All teachers who are new to the GUHSD participate in the program their first three years.

Is participation of new teachers voluntary or mandatory?

Participation is mandatory. Much of the professional conversation in the GUHSD schools is regarding the Essential Elements of Instruction. Experienced teachers, as well as teachers new to the profession, need to be familiar with the work of Madeline Hunter.

Who provides the mentoring/induction?

The mentoring team inducts new teachers.

What are the criteria for being a mentor?

Teachers need to be experienced in the GUHSD schools, master teachers, and very familiar with the Essential Elements of Instruction.

What are the job responsibilities of the mentor?

Mentors work with teachers in their first three years of employment in GUHSD. Mentors observe teachers and do cognitive coaching with them. In addition, they offer workshops in the schools, as well as for the district, on curriculum and instruction.

Is peer observation and coaching a requirement of mentors?

Yes, observation and cognitive coaching are required.

Do mentors have full-time classroom teaching responsibilities?

Mentors teach two classes a day, and are released from teaching the other three periods to mentor new teachers.

How are mentors selected?

Experienced teachers are invited to apply to be in a pool of trained mentors. They go through a screening process that includes observing a lesson taught by another teacher, scripting and then analyzing it. In addition, they submit a videotape of themselves teaching a lesson. They are also interviewed. If they are accepted into the pool of mentors, they are then able to apply if a position becomes available at one of the schools.

If an opening occurs, the principal interviews mentors from the pool who applied, and selects one for the position. Preference is given, all things being equal, to a master teacher who works in the school in which there is the opening. It has been found that familiarity with school culture is important knowledge to have as the mentor in that building.

Are mentors paid?

Mentors are paid a teacher's salary.

How are matches made between mentors and new teachers?

Mentors work with all new teachers in their building regardless of content area. With the increase in hiring, they work with about 23 new teachers on each local campus.

Are mentors trained?

Norman Smalley formerly trained the mentors. When Norman became an assistant principal, it was decided that the mentors would cross-train, and they rose to a new level of expertise.

Who supervises mentors?

Vernon Jacobs supervises the mentors.

What supports are available for mentors?

Is there professional staff development for the mentors?

Mentors train each other, sharing different areas of expertise. They meet at the district office every Friday to support each other, plan together, and train each other.

Who provides it?

In addition to the mentors, consultants are sometimes hired to do specific training with mentors.

What resources are available for mentors?

Mentors have each other, consultants, and the district administrators as resources.

Do mentors evaluate new teachers?

No, mentors never evaluate new teachers.

Is the mentor/new teacher relationship confidential?

Mentors never speak with administrators about the performance of new teachers. An administrator may tell a mentor that she or he told the new teacher to work with the mentor on a specific skill or issue, and may ask the mentor if the teacher followed up with the mentor. The mentor could answer that kind of question, as long as there wasn't any discussion of the teacher's performance.

What are the resources required for the program?

1. Mentor salaries (including benefits) $298,080
2. Regular workshops for first-,
   second-, and third-year teachers $94,457
3. Summer workshops for first-, second-,
   and third-year teachers $178,013
4. Books, pamphlets, publications $4,025
5. Materials $1,000

Funding

The funding is from the district budget.

Who requests the funding?

Vernon Jacobs requests the funding for the program.

Evaluation of the Program

How is the program evaluated?

The first-, second-, and third-year teachers are surveyed about the program. The mentor team and Vernon carefully consider the teachers' feedback about the program and their experience being mentored in an effort to improve the program based on what is said in the survey.

Who sees the results?

The results are shared at meetings with the school board and are therefore available to the public.

Recruitment, Hiring, and Retention of New Staff

How many new teachers are recruited and hired?

Sixty to 100 new teachers are hired each year.

Is there any data that correlates the mentoring program with the retention of new teachers?

Teacher retention in the Glendale Union High School District has improved substantially since the implementation of the mentor program. A 10-year analysis reveals the following:

1. Thirty-two percent of the teachers hired in 1991, prior to implementation of the mentor program, remained within the district for 10 years. These percentages increased to 55 percent for those teachers hired in 1992, the first year of the program implementation.
2. Forty-seven percent of teachers hired in 1991, prior to implementation of the mentor program, remained within the district for five years. Since the program was implemented in 1992, this percentage has ranged from 53 percent to 80 percent.

3. The percentage of teachers remaining within the district between five and ten years is substantially larger for those who participated in the mentor program than for those who did not.

What are the indicators of program success?

Personnel at GUHSD believe they are successfully retaining quality teachers, and the data supports that belief. It appears that teachers who need to be counseled out of teaching are identified earlier in their teaching careers.

NEWPORT NEWS PUBLIC SCHOOLS
INSTRUCTIONAL MENTORING PROGRAM
NEWPORT NEWS, VIRGINIA

Kathleen Pietrasanta, Director of Instructional Mentoring
12465 Warwick Boulevard
Newport News, Virginia 23606
757-591-4584
kpietras@sbo.nn.k12.va.us
As of July 9, 2001

Phil Hamilton, Coordinator of Funding and Site-Based Programs
12465 Warwick Boulevard
Newport News, Virginia 23606
757-591-7436
phamilto@sbo.nn.k12.va.us
As of July 9, 2001

DEMOGRAPHICS

The following figures are for the 2000-2001 school year.

Grade Levels	Pre K-12	Urban/Suburban/Rural	Urban
Student Population	33,000	Ethnic Makeup* African American Asian American Caucasian Hispanic Native American	54% 2% 39% 4% 1%
Teacher Population	2,350	% New Teachers	15%
		Per Pupil Expenditure	$5,500

* The statistics available from the district delineated the ethnic makeup as shown.
  There was no information about students of more than one racial heritage.

The following information was obtained from telephone conversations and e-mail correspondence with Phil Hamilton and Kathleen Pietrasanta.

MENTOR PROGRAM

Unique Feature of Program	PATHWISE induction program	Mentoring Is/ Is Not Mandated for Certification/ Licensing	Is mandated
Cognitive Coaching Is/ Is Not a Component	Is a component	Mentors Do/Do Not Evaluate the New Teachers With Whom They Work	Do not evaluate
Cost of Program	$96,280	Funding	Local and State
Mentors Are Full-Time/ Part-Time Teachers	Full-time	Mentor Remuneration	$500
Program in Existence	PATHWISE: 2 years; Other mentor programs: 9 years	Duration of Program for New Teachers	1 year, possibly 2 years, if recommended by the principal
Higher Education Affiliation	None	Program Coordinator	Kathleen Pietrasanta: Instructional Mentoring; Phil Hamilton: funding and site-based coordination

History

In 1997–1998, Educational Testing Service (ETS) field-tested the PATHWISE materials. Newport News became one of the first divisions to have an internal trainer, rather than having one of the ETS trainers come to their site. Charlotte Danielson had worked with educators in Newport News to set up their evaluation system, so using the PATH-WISE induction program seemed like a natural continuation of the relationship. It also provided alignment between the way new teachers would be evaluated and the way new teachers would be supported.

State Mandates

Is mentoring mandated for new teachers?
Yes.

Is mentoring part of certification or licensure?
No.

Is funding provided to support the mandate?
Yes. The commonwealth provides $5,075,000 per year to support its mentoring/clinical faculty program. Localities may apply for state mentor grants and are required to provide a 50 percent match if they are awarded the grant.

Goals

- Provide a structured support system for novice teachers
- Train individuals to be the backbone of the support for novice teachers
- Recruit and retain new teachers

Program Design

What are the components and recommended schedule of the program?
There are five different programs to mentor new teachers. Novice teachers participate in some of them, depending on their specialty and decisions of the building administrators.

1. PATHWISE is the main program, offered through the department of professional development. It is not a mandated program. Principals may recommend teachers from their building for training, and in so doing, involve their new teachers in the PATHWISE induction program. The district is working towards having trained PATHWISE mentors in every building so that ultimately it is the primary program for all novice teachers.
2. Site-based mentoring programs are available in schools where the principals haven't chosen to participate in PATHWISE.

These site-based programs meet the state mandate. Site-based programs are designed by schools and submitted to the professional development department for funding. They receive $100/novice teacher for those programs.

3. The special education department provides Peer Partners; they match new special education teachers with veteran teachers to help the novices become more knowledgeable of special education regulations and more skillful in writing IEPs.

4. The Minority Male Mentorship Program was started by the human resources department about 7 years ago to address the difficulty in attracting minority male teachers. The program holds monthly meetings before the school day begins, as a support group and for specialized programs.

5. The elementary instructional department offers the Helping Hands Mentorship Program. This is for 50 elementary novice teachers who meet quarterly, for two hours after school, to deal with instructional strategies and classroom management techniques. This program is a way for schools that don't participate in the PATHWISE program to meet the state requirement.

6. Every new teacher receives *First Days of School* by Harry Wong.

7. New Teacher Orientation is 5 days in August, the week before the other teachers report. The days are devoted to the following topics: Human Resources (1), Instructional Services (2), Administrative and Alternative Services (1), Building Based (1).

The PATHWISE induction program provides an ongoing process of structured learning and thinking about teaching. There are ten events, some of which take one to three hours to complete, and others of which last for two to six weeks. These are:

1. Teaching Environment Profile
2. Inquiry 1—Establishing a Learning Environment
3. Profile of Practice 1
4. Individual Growth Plans 1 & 2
5. Profile of Practice 2
6. Inquiry 2—Developing Instructional Experiences
7. Inquiry 3—Analysis of Student Work
8. Assessment and Summary of Professional Growth
9. Colloquium

Mentors are required to do a minimum of two rounds of observations of the novice teacher.

Are there any programs that complement the mentor program?

No.

Who designed the mentor program?

The PATHWISE induction program was developed by Educational Testing Service and is based on the work of Charlotte Danielson. In the Newport News public school system, this program is referred to as Instructional Mentoring. It is implemented according to the recommendations of ETS.

Program Administration

Who coordinates the mentor program?

Kathleen Pietrasanta is the professional development department's coordinator of the Instructional Mentoring Program. Phil Hamilton does the fiscal and site-based coordination.

How is information communicated to shareholders?

Building principals were made aware of the state requirements. If they recommend teachers for training as instructional mentors in the PATHWISE induction program, their new teachers may participate in the Instructional Mentoring Program. If not, they have the other options listed above.

Who coordinates the integration of the mentor program with other professional development opportunities/requirements in the school/ district?

There are three coordinators and a director of the professional development department. Kathleen is the lead coordinator to work with other department members in integrating other professional development opportunities.

Participants

Who is served?

Novice teachers who have never taught before are the teachers in the PATHWISE program. Experienced teachers who are new to the district are supported in their buildings.

Is participation of new teachers voluntary or mandatory?

The novice teacher must participate in whatever the teacher's school has chosen for its mentoring program. If a school has selected Instructional Mentoring as its mentoring program, then the novice teacher is mandated to participate.

Who provides the mentoring/induction?

Classroom teachers are the mentors in the Instructional Mentoring Program.

What are the criteria for being a mentor?

Principal recommendation and participation in the 4-day training in PATHWISE are the criteria for becoming a mentor.

What are the job responsibilities of the mentor?

The responsibilities of mentors are to provide support for, and coaching on, the new teacher's performance using the structured events of the PATHWISE program.

Is peer observation and coaching a requirement of mentors?

Yes.

Do mentors have full-time classroom teaching responsibilities?

Yes.

How are mentors available to participate in the program?

Mentors meet with novice teachers before and/or after school. Sometimes principals schedule common planning time. The mentors and the principals work out the coverage at the building level.

How are mentors selected?

Everyone who is recommended by a principal and agrees to do the 4-day PATHWISE training is selected and trained.

Are mentors paid?

Yes. This year they were paid $500 stipends.

How are matches made between mentors and new teachers?

The principals match the mentors with the new teachers. Ideally it is someone at the same grade level or subject area and in close proximity within the building.

Are mentors trained?

Mentors attend 4 days (24 hours) of summer training. Certified PATHWISE trainers conduct the 4-day training.

Who supervises mentors?

Principals supervise the mentors, as they do all teachers in their buildings, in accordance with the responsibilities of their roles. Principals make sure that mentors implement the PATHWISE events with the novice teachers. If they have any concerns, they speak with Kathleen.

What supports are available for mentors?

Is there professional development for the mentors?

There are other professional development opportunities for all teachers in the division, and the mentors may choose to participate.

Who provides it?

The professional development department, as well as other departments, provide the professional development.

What resources are available for mentors?

Mentors receive the PATHWISE box of structured activities.

Do mentors evaluate new teachers?

No.

Is the mentor/new teacher relationship confidential?

Yes. Mentor teachers may share information if the novice teacher gives permission for them to do so.

What are the resources required for the Instructional Mentoring Program?

101 novice teachers participated in the program in 2000–2001.

1. Mentor training: Three training cycles during the summer (75 mentors are trained each year, and may continue to serve in future years) $ 7,200
2. New teacher orientation: Food during the week-long orientation $12,000

3. Colloquium dinner	$3,780
4. Materials:	
PATHWISE box of activities	$22,000
The First Days of School	$8,000
5. Stipends for mentors	$50,500
6. Substitutes for released time (worked out within the building—classes are covered internally)	Varies

Funding

What are the funding sources?

The district funds the program, with some support from the state. In 2000–2001, the state awarded a grant of $35,000.

Who requests the funding?

Phil is responsible for completing the application for state mentoring funds.

Evaluation of the Program

How is the program evaluated?

At the end of the year, novice teachers, mentors, and principals complete evaluation forms. Christopher Newport University tabulates the results.

Who sees the results?

The professional development department reviews the results of the surveys.

Recruitment, Hiring, and Retention of New Staff

How many new teachers are recruited and hired?

In 2000–2001, 400 new teachers were hired. In 2001–2002, 500 teachers are anticipated.

Is there any data that correlates the mentoring program with the retention of new teachers?

As of 2001, there is little data that indicates the long-term success of the Instructional Mentoring Program as it has only been in existence for two years. Newport News has partnered with Educational Testing Service to evaluate the effectiveness of the program. This research project is in its beginning stages. Data collected will be related to teacher retention, job satisfaction and self-efficacy, classroom practice, and student learning.

In addition, the Consortium for Policy Research in Education, based at the University of Wisconsin–Madison, has conducted additional research into the Instructional Mentoring Program. The results of that study have not yet been released.

What are the indicators of program success?

Of the 78 mentors who were assigned to novice teachers the first year instructional mentoring was implemented, 55 of them also mentored during the second year; this is a 70 percent retention rate for mentors.

The following anecdotal data was gathered from active mentors:

Impact on the assigned novice teacher

"It has helped to improve her teaching qualities in each of the four domains. Just being available to answer questions and share materials was a relief."

"She was totally overwhelmed with the 'extra' side of teaching (paperwork, phone calls, conferences, etc.), and the mentoring experience has had a profound effect on her ability to handle it."

Impact on the mentor

"Helping a new teacher has been very rewarding."

"It has taken up every possible minute of my day. It forces me to take more time during the evening to do my own work."

Impact on the students

"I have mixed feelings. . . . I have had to spend time away from the classroom to observe. On the other hand, I am more conscious of incorporating items that I am suggesting to my mentee."

"My students reaped the benefit of the mentoring experience. It made me more aware of their differences and learning styles.

When we planned our lessons, . . . they were developed for them to meet with success."

Insights into professional growth

"When you help someone professionally, it is always very rewarding. It makes you dig in deep and reflect more about how you have evolved over the years. Others . . . have shared with me and now it is my turn to pass it on."

"I am reviewing the qualities of the effective teacher, so that is a positive reminder to me as a professional."

Changes I will make in my next instructional mentoring experience

". . . begin immediately and help the new teacher start with a good shoulder to lean on."

FRANCIS HOWELL SCHOOL DISTRICT
MENTORING PROGRAM
SAINT CHARLES, MISSOURI

Chris Guinther, Professional Development Chairperson
4545 Central School Road
Saint Charles, Missouri 63304
636-398-4581
mosped@aol.com
As of June 30, 2001

DEMOGRAPHICS

The following figures are for the 2000-2001 school year.

Grade Levels	K-12	Urban/Suburban/Rural	Suburban
Student Population	18,523	Ethnic Makeup* African American Asian American Caucasian Latino/a	3.0% 0.8% 93.9% 0.3%
Teacher Population	1,442	% New Teachers	4.2%
		Per Pupil Expenditure	$5,744

* The statistics available from the district delineated the ethnic makeup as shown.
  There was no information about students of more than one racial heritage.

The following information was obtained from telephone conversations and e-mail correspondence with Chris Guinther, as well as quoted from written materials distributed in the program.

History

This mentoring program was created when the Excellence in Education Act was passed in Missouri in 1985, effective in 1988.

MENTOR PROGRAM

Unique Feature of Program	Part-time mentors work with a professional development committee and school administrators to support new teachers	Mentoring Is/ Is Not Mandated for Certification/ Licensing	Is mandated
Cognitive Coaching Is/ Is Not a Component	Is a component	Mentors Do/Do Not Evaluate the New Teachers With Whom They Work	Do not evaluate
Cost of Program	$47,295 + $2,500 for the Beginning Teacher Network	Funding	District
Mentors Are Full-Time/ Part-Time Teachers	Full-time	Mentor Remuneration	$350 per year
Program in Existence	15 years	Duration of Program for New Teachers	1 year, possibly 2
Higher Education Affiliation	Lindenwood University	Program Coordinator	Chris Guinther

State Mandates

Is mentoring mandated for new teachers?

Yes, mentoring is mandated for new teachers in Missouri.

Is mentoring part of certification or licensure?

Yes, part of the certification requirement for first-year teachers is that they be mentored during their first year, and that a mentoring program be available in their second year, if necessary. The state requirements for licensure involve a three-stage process: Professional Certificates I, II, and Continuous Professional Certificate (CPC). The mentoring program, and the district-developed Beginning Teacher Network, are ways for new teachers to meet some of these requirements.

Is funding provided to support the mandate?

When the Excellence in Education Act was implemented in 1988, no money had been mandated for its implementation in the local school districts. Funding to support the mandate of mentoring new teachers was provided in 1993, when the Outstanding Schools Act was passed. It mandated that 1 percent of state funding be spent on professional development, with a professional development committee in each school system, in collaboration with the administration and approval by the school board, making the decisions about professional development and the allocation of those funds. The Excellence in Education Act had mandated that a professional development committee (PDC) be formed in each school district, and that its members be elected by the teachers. A school system's state funding could be jeopardized if it didn't follow the stipulations of the Outstanding Schools Act.

Goals

The purpose of the mentoring program is to provide new teachers a collegial relationship that will give positive reinforcement to new ideas, help them gain self-confidence and allow them to become self-directed individuals.

Program Design

What are the components and recommended schedule of the program?

Each new teacher is assigned a mentor for her/his first year of teaching. There is the possibility for a second year of mentoring. In addition to required meetings with mentors, there is the Beginning Teacher Network (BTN) which meets monthly after school on a voluntary basis.

The recommended components and schedule of the mentor program are:

- One day of mentor training, usually in the spring or summer and ideally before the mentoring starts, with follow-up at BTN meetings and at the building and individual level.
- A two-day orientation for new teachers before school starts. It is planned by the administration. The curriculum and instruction facilitators offer the program.

- Quarterly meetings of a mentoring triad, which works during the first six weeks of school to establish the professional development plan, and throughout the year to monitor it. This triad is composed of a principal, the mentor, and the new teacher. The principal is expected to keep mentoring separate from evaluation.
- Weekly meetings of the mentor and mentee.
- A BTN meeting of mentors and mentees during the first quarter.
- Classroom observations and at least one peer observation during the year, supported by up to three released days per partnership.
- End-of-year tea to celebrate the new teachers' first year and those who supported them.
- Ideally, the partnership develops into a peer coaching/peer support model, embedded into the school routine.

The program begins when the mentor and new teacher are matched, hopefully shortly after the new teacher is hired. Ideally this happens before school starts, so that the mentor may assist the new teacher in becoming familiar with the building, personnel, and other resources, as well as district expectations and some best practices for use with students and parents during the first few weeks of school.

The program historically finishes at the end of the school year, though teachers often continue the relationship they developed. Occasionally teachers may request a second year of mentoring, which would take the form of released days for the teacher and mentor to work together.

Are there any programs that complement the mentor program?

The Beginning Teacher Network meets monthly after school, for 75 minutes. The meetings are an opportunity for new teachers to get to know each other and share their experiences and concerns. Workshops are also offered at each meeting, based on a needs assessment that is conducted at the beginning of the year. These workshops are often on topics including: classroom management, parent conferencing, dealing with difficult people, student motivation, differentiated instruction, time management, and curriculum and instruction issues. Voluntary participation in the network fulfills another of the state's certification requirements, which is to participate in a beginning teacher assistance program provided through a college or university. The Francis Howell School District (FHSD) affiliated with

Lindenwood University, and the BTN was approved as an option for this certification requirement.

In addition, the BTN affords new teachers the opportunity to meet confidentially with the facilitators and coordinators, who are other experienced teachers.

Who designed the program?

A position was created by the superintendent when the Outstanding Schools Act was implemented, and part of the job description included evaluating, supporting, and overseeing the mentor program for new teachers, as well as establishing some new support systems for first-year teachers. BTN was an idea that Chris Guinther got from other NEA affiliates. Chris started it at the FHSD. A portion of the mentor program coordinator's salary was paid for by the school district. The money that is provided through the Outstanding Schools Act stipulates that certain positions may not be funded by it, including administrators of any programs.

Program Administration

Who coordinates the mentor program?

Chris Guinther, a curriculum and instruction facilitator, coordinates the mentor program as part of her job responsibilities. Chris, a former teacher and active member of the Francis Howell Education Association (FHEA), is paid a teacher's salary, showing a symbolic alignment with the new teachers as a peer. Chris was appointed for the 1993–1994 school year. It had been decided that a teacher from within the district would be most able to support new teachers as a confidential consultant, as well as work with district personnel, with many of whom she or he had relationships. The director of curriculum and instruction supervises Chris and all curriculum and instruction facilitators.

Chris coordinates the mentor training, as well as the meetings of mentors and mentees. In addition, she designs and facilitates the BTN meetings.

How is information communicated to shareholders?

Teacher candidates learn of the program after they are hired, when they receive a letter from Chris through her role as coordinator of the mentor program. Other teachers know about the program, based on an introduction that was made when it was created. Facilitators and building and district PDCs tell current staff about the program.

Chris meets with the administrators at least once a year to speak with them about the mentor program, and to underscore the intent and protocols of the program. She also facilitates the district PDC and is a resource to building PDCs.

Who coordinates the integration of the mentor program with other professional development opportunities/requirements in the school/ district?

The PDC plans and oversees all professional development in the district, and coordinates the integration of the mentor program with other professional development opportunities and requirements of the district, as is required by the Excellence in Education Act. The PDC works closely with the curriculum and instruction facilitators.

Participants

Who is served?

The program is designed for first-year teachers, who are required to participate in mentoring. In addition, second-year teachers and those who are new to the district or their position may apply for informal mentoring with an experienced teacher. This opportunity, called "Mentoring Beyond the First Year," is for teachers who would benefit from continued mentoring, opportunities for peer coaching or collaboration.

Is participation of new teachers voluntary or mandatory?

Participation of new teachers is mandatory.

Who provides the mentoring/induction?

Mentors, who are classroom teachers, provide the mentoring.

What are the criteria for being a mentor?

- Five years of teaching experience
- Well versed in district/building policy and procedures.
- Substantial experience in classroom instruction

- Demonstrated exemplary teaching ability, including subject-matter knowledge, and mastery of a range of teaching strategies to meet the needs of all students.
- Effective communication skills
- Committed to the concept of lifelong learning and personal professional development
- Interested in guiding new teachers
- Able to communicate and respond to a new teacher's needs
- Aware of peer coaching techniques and have participated in peer coaching training

What are the job responsibilities of being a mentor?

Mentors sign a "Mentor Agreement" in which they agree to assume the following responsibilities:

- Serving as a confidential consultant to their mentee
- Meeting at least weekly with their mentee
- Meeting at least quarterly with the mentoring triad
- Assisting the mentor triad in writing, implementing, and evaluating the professional development plan (PDP) and keeping a copy of that plan
- Providing opportunities for the mentee to observe in the mentor's classroom or in other classrooms
- Participating in at least one peer coaching activity in the mentee's classroom
- Keeping an updated record of the work the mentee and mentor did together
- Familiarizing the mentee with the district, building, and department policies and procedures
- Attending the mentor-mentee BTN meeting on writing the PDP

Is peer observation and coaching required of mentors?

Yes. In addition to informal observations, at least one observation and conference is required during the year.

Do mentors have full-time classroom teaching responsibilities?

Yes, mentors are full-time classroom teachers.

How are mentors available to participate in the program?

Mentors are paid a substitute stipend ($75) if they attend a training session during non-contractual time. Otherwise the PDC pays for the substitute. Up to three days of released time is provided for each mentor and new teacher pair to meet. If they meet during non-contractual time, mentors may be compensated at the rate substitutes are paid, which is $75 a day.

How are mentors selected?

Mentors volunteer for the role, and are sometimes invited to volunteer. Mentors are chosen by the principal, grade level or department chair, and building representative from the PDC.

Are mentors paid?

Yes, mentors are paid $350 a year.

How are matches made between mentors and new teachers?

Chris Guinther writes to teachers as soon as they are hired, welcoming them and telling them about the mentor program. The building principals, grade-level or department chairs, and district PDC representatives meet to match new teachers and their mentors. Sometimes any of these people may suggest that a teacher be a mentor for a new teacher, with the understanding that mentoring is a voluntary role.

Are mentors trained?

Mentors are trained on an as-needed basis, usually in the spring or summer.

Who supervises mentors?

District PDC representatives, principals, and curriculum and instruction facilitators all provide support for mentors. The district PDC and curriculum and instruction department are ultimately responsible for the mentoring program.

What supports are available for mentors?

Is there professional development for the mentors?

Yes. Mentors receive one day of mentor training, usually before they begin mentoring.

Who provides it?

Chris, the other curriculum and instruction facilitators, and other school personnel provide training.

What resources are available for mentors?

Curriculum and instruction facilitators consult with mentors as needed.

Do mentors evaluate new teachers?

No, mentors do not evaluate new teachers.

Is the mentor/new teacher relationship confidential?

Yes. It is completely confidential, except in cases where the mentor perceives that students are at risk being in the new teacher's classroom, in which case the mentor is to report that situation to a building supervisor.

What are the resources required for the program?

- Mentor training $2,500
- Food for conferences and meetings $1,100
- Materials:
  Printing for the orientation, new teacher
  notebooks, and mentor notebooks $1,175
- Stipends for mentors at $350/mentor $23,520
- Substitutes for released time:
  $10,000 first year;
  $9,000 second year $19,000
- Program director's salary:
  A portion of Chris's salary
  for direction of program $20,000

A $2000 grant was awarded by the state department to get additional released time and support for new special education teachers in the 2001–2002 school year.

The Beginning Teacher Network costs are:

- Meeting expenses $2,500
  In addition to typical expenditures, door prizes are given at each meeting. These include school supplies and books for new teachers.

Funding

The PDC is allocated at least 1 percent of the money the school receives from the state. For the year 2000, the PDC allocation for support of the mentor program for first- and second-year teachers amounted to $45,020. The PDC contributed $1,500 to the BTN, and the Francis Howell Education Association contributed $1,000 to support the BTN. The district contributed the portion of Chris's salary that corresponded to the portion of her job that was devoted to mentoring and inducting new teachers.

Who requests the funding?

The district PDC budgeting process takes place in late winter/early spring. The PDC recognizes the need to support those new to the profession; the mentoring program and the BTN are priority-funding items. The local association also realizes the importance of the program and generously has funded the requests from the facilitator. This takes place in spring.

Evaluation of the Program

What is the evaluation process?

Chris conducts annual evaluations by sending written evaluation forms to mentors, new teachers, and principals at the end of the school year. She also meets with the principals during the school year to hear their feedback, and has a meeting with the mentors and mentees to hear their perceptions of the program. The BTN is another time when she may hear how the teachers feel their mentors are supporting them. Using the district e-mail system, new teachers are frequently updated on issues and asked for their feedback.

Who sees the results?

Chris reports her findings to the administration and the PDC, through the professional development plan evaluation process.

Recruitment, Hiring, and Retention of New Staff

How many new teachers are recruited and hired?

New teachers are being hired in large numbers. Some years there are as many as 90 first-year teachers. In 2000–2001, there were 60 new teachers in the district.

Is there any information correlating the mentoring program with the retention of new teachers?

New teachers are seeking employment elsewhere because of the current, difficult financial situation of the district. Questions are being added to the exit interviews regarding mentoring to assess its impact on teachers.

What are the indicators of program success?

Satisfaction of mentees, mentors, and principals with the program all indicate the success of the program. One new teacher reported that she didn't think she would have survived the year if it hadn't been for the program and her mentor.

Saint Paul Public Schools Learning Circles/ Mentor Program for New Teachers Saint Paul, Minnesota

Jeanne Klein, Director of Staff Development
1001 Johnson Parkway
Saint Paul, Minnesota 55106
651-793-5472
Fax: 651-793-5490
jeanne.klein@spps.org
As of July 9, 2001

DEMOGRAPHICS

The following figures are for the 1999-2000 school year.

Grade Levels	K-12	Urban/Suburban/Rural	Urban
Student Population	46,000	Ethnic Makeup* American Indian Hispanic African American Asian American White	 1.9% 8.9% 22.7% 31.2% 35.1%
Teacher Population	3,700	% New Teachers	8%
		Per Pupil Expenditure	$9,500

* The statistics available from the district delineated the ethnic makeup as shown.
 There was no information about students of more than one racial heritage.

The following information was obtained from telephone conversations with Jeanne Klein, or is quoted from printed written materials distributed in the program.

History

Mentoring had been provided to new teachers through large orientation meetings, with 300 new teachers in attendance. It was evident that they were leaving these meetings with a high degree of angst

MENTOR PROGRAM

Unique Feature of Program	Small groups of teachers meet monthly with a resource colleague to discuss issues of their choosing	Mentoring Is/ Is Not Mandated for Certification/ Licensing	Is not mandated
Cognitive Coaching Is/Is Not a Component	Is not required	Mentors Do/Do Not Evaluate the New Teachers With Whom They Work	Do not evaluate
Cost of Program	$362,565	Funding	District, grant, and union
Mentors Are Full-Time/Part-Time Teachers	Full-time	Mentor Remuneration	$3,000 for resource colleagues; $250-300 for building mentors
Program in Existence	3 years	Duration of Program for New Teachers	3 years
Higher Education Affiliation	Hamline University	Program Coordinator	Jeanne Klein

about classroom management and other impending issues. Jeanne Klein and staff development colleagues knew that they needed to break the new teachers into smaller groups and provide ongoing support. There were eight staff members in the staff development office, and they couldn't do it all. Jeanne Klein, the director, charged them with thinking of a way to do this. Conversations with Walter Enloe about Learning Circles, and ideas Jeanne Klein had about resource colleagues were the beginning of the program that is now in place.

State Mandates

Is mentoring mandated for new teachers?
No.

Is mentoring part of certification or licensure?
No.

Is funding provided to support the mandate?
No.

Goals

The primary goal of staff development's Learning Circles/Mentor Program (LC/M Program) is creating a positive environment for new teachers that will ensure their continuous professional growth. This program is a research-based program with an emphasis on group work, team building, and "quality circles" communities of learning. The Saint Paul LC/M Program is based on the six-strand theory using the learning circles concept to support new teachers. The following are the six key conditions: build community with other learners; construct knowledge through personal experiences; support other learners; document reflections on one's own experience; assess expectations; improve the class culture.

The LC/M Program creates a process of apprenticeship for new teachers, creates a structure to communicate and support new teachers, formalizes support for implementation, assessment and reflection of best practices, and aligns with state and national standards for new teacher training. The motto is: "Never send anyone alone."

Program Design

What are the components and recommended schedule of the program?

- The Learning Circles Program is for teachers in their first year of teaching in the Saint Paul public schools.
- Before school starts, there are two days of welcome and orientation for new teachers.
- Resource colleagues participate in those days as small-group facilitators.
- Every month a resource colleague meets with five to ten new teachers, preferably from the same school, to facilitate a two-hour learning circle. The dates and times of these before- or afterschool meetings are set by the group.

- New teachers are paid $16.50 an hour to attend these two-hour meetings each month of their first year. They are paid for up to 3 hours a month for participation in the program. They may continue meeting after their first year without any remuneration.
- The agenda for the Learning Circles meetings are largely determined by the new teachers. Sometimes a resource colleague will alert new teachers to upcoming events or give suggestions about ways to prepare for upcoming responsibilities.
- Resource colleagues consult with teachers individually to develop an action plan.
- Resource colleagues are available to videotape new teachers and give them confidential, nonevaluative feedback on their teaching.
- If a new teacher does not teach in the same school as her/his resource colleague, the new teacher is also assigned a mentor who teaches in the same school.
- Resource colleagues receive training and support, and have an end of the year celebration

Are there any programs that complement the mentor program?

There is an Information Fair held before school for new teachers. Different school system departments are represented, including food service, transportation, and human resources. In addition, the Chamber of Commerce and other city resources have tables at the fair. Candy and other prizes are given away at these tables, encouraging new teachers to get as much information as possible.

Who designed the mentor program?

The Learning Circles/Mentor Program for first-year teachers was developed by teachers who were working in the office of staff development on special assignment, under the direction of Jeanne Klein. Staff members worked with Walter Enloe, a professor at Hamline University, to understand Learning Circles and then adapt it.

Program Administration

Who coordinates the mentor program?

Nancy Hall coordinates the program, as part of the department of staff development, which is directed by Jeanne Klein.

How is information communicated to shareholders?

Nancy Hall and Jeanne Klein communicate with shareholders in the school community.

Who coordinates the integration of the mentor program with other professional development opportunities/requirements in the school/ district?

Nancy Hall and Jeanne Klein, in collaboration with others members of the staff in the department of staff development, coordinate the Learning Circles/Mentor Program with other staff development in the system.

Participants

Who is served?

Teachers in their first year of teaching in the Saint Paul public schools are in the Learning Circles Program.

Is participation of new teachers voluntary or mandatory?

Participation is mandatory. It is a contractual requirement that new teachers devote seven days to induction.

Who provides the mentoring/induction?

Resource colleagues, who are full-time teaching colleagues, facilitate the Learning Circles and do peer observation and review. In addition, there are building-based mentors, also full-time teaching colleagues, for any teacher whose resource colleague is not in the same school she or he is working in.

What are the criteria for being a resource colleague?

The criteria to be a resource colleague are:

- A tenured Saint Paul public school teacher with at least 5 years of classroom experience, currently assigned teaching responsibilities
- Evidence of successful teaching in a K-12 classroom
- Evidence of successful mentoring

In addition, the preferred criteria are:

- Evidence of successful mentoring in the Saint Paul Federation of Teachers mentoring program
- Evidence of successful group facilitation
- Evidence of training in cognitive coaching or peer assistance review
- Commitment to the principles of the Urban Learner Framework
- Knowledge of the Minnesota State Graduation Standards
- Knowledge of the New Teacher Induction program

What are the job responsibilities of the resource colleague?

- Provide leadership with small groups of educators new to Saint Paul by assisting them in identifying and articulating professional development needs
- Offer quality, ongoing, experiential, professional development that comes as close to replicating the work of their own teaching
- Attend and participate fully in all training sessions and monthly, cluster-level, afterschool meetings, beginning August 23
- Be part of a learning community as a teacher/learner
- Arrange for and facilitate "Homebase/Learning Circle Meetings" with educators new to Saint Paul at least twice monthly
- Attend support sessions for resource colleagues
- Work with new teachers in one-on-one mentoring situations with Learning Circle teachers when needed

Is peer observation and coaching required of the mentor?

Observation and coaching is not required, though many new teachers request and welcome the feedback. Resource colleagues are trained in viewing videotapes to give feedback, and there are substitutes available for resource colleagues to do observations and conferencing when requested.

If a teacher is having difficulty, a principal may ask the resource colleague to observe and share objective data. Judgmental statements by the resource colleague are not expected.

Do resource colleagues/mentors have full-time classroom teaching responsibilities?

Yes.

How are resource colleagues available to participate in the program?

Resource colleagues may apply for substitutes to cover them when they observe/videotape new teachers. They are also released to attend training that is held during the school day. Other trainings occur before school, and the Learning Circles are scheduled outside of the school day.

How are resource colleagues/mentors selected?

Resource colleagues are interviewed and selected by staff members in the department of staff development, directed by Jeanne Klein.

New teachers may choose their own mentors for their second and third year.

Are resource colleagues/mentors paid?

Yes. Resource colleagues are able to earn up to an additional $3,000 during the school year for work with groups of new teachers at least twice monthly.

Mentors earn between $250 and $300 during the school year.

Mentors of teachers in their second and third year receive $600 a year. The Saint Paul Federation of Teachers pays half the costs for the mentor stipends.

How are matches made between mentors and new teachers?

Learning Circles are typically composed of new teachers from the same building. Occasionally, job-alike groups are formed at the participants' request, such as groups of nurses, social workers, and special education teachers. The system prefers that specialists are part of other Learning Circles, yet honors requests they make to be together.

Teachers in their second and third year may select their own mentor, and that request is honored if agreeable to the mentor.

Are resource colleagues trained?

Yes. The Saint Paul Learning Circles/Mentor Program has formalized a collaboration with Hamline University. The six essential conditions were recreated in a Learning Circles course designed by Walter Enloe and Nancy Hall. Hamline University credits (Professional Educational Development Seminar) were offered to any new teacher, resource colleague, master mentor teacher, or other staff member who would take responsibility for their own professional development through this learning concept. Jeanne Klein and Nancy Hall have negotiated a collaborative effort with Hamline University's Center for Excellence in Urban Teaching to provide strategic practices for new teachers in their classrooms in the 2001–2002 school year. This will provide background information for resource colleagues to involve new teachers in the development of instructional techniques that incorporate cultural learning styles.

There is training after school for resource colleagues to learn to assess teaching from videotapes. The national board procedures for observing videotaped classroom teaching are used.

Who supervises resource colleagues/mentors?

Personnel from the staff development department supervise and support resource colleagues.

What supports are available for resource colleagues/mentors?

Is there professional development for the resource colleagues/mentors?

There are afterschool sessions for the resource colleagues on issues they need to discuss. In addition, there is a course at Hamline University about Learning Circles. This course is not mandatory training for the resource colleagues. If they opt to take it, they pay a reduced rate for the course credits and take the course on the school campus.

Who provides it?

Jeanne and Nancy facilitate the afterschool sessions. The course on Learning Circles is offered at Hamline University.

What resources are available for resource colleagues?

- An end-of-year retreat
- Meetings with Jeanne and/or Nancy
- Video cameras
- Technology
- A CD-ROM on classroom management
- A resource guide
- Grants for graduate credit
- Released days and planning time
- Ongoing training in peer coaching
- A retreat day

Do resource colleagues evaluate new teachers?

No, according to their contracts, resource colleagues may not evaluate. They do give feedback to new teachers after the observation.

Is the mentor/new teacher relationship confidential?

Yes, it is confidential.

What are the resources required for the program?

- Mentor training and new teacher orientation $80,000
- Stipends for resource colleagues
  at $3,000 per year per resource colleague $90,000
- Stipends for mentors in years
  2 and 3 at $600/year $133,200
- Stipends for building mentors in year
  one at $250–300 per year per mentor   Varies
- Compensation to new teachers for
  participation in meetings at $16.50/hour
  for 3 hours/month $16,965
- Mentees get salary scale credit for
  attendance at meetings   Varies
- Substitutes for released time $12,000
- Hardware/audiovisual equipment $25,000
- Resource guides, 300 at $18/guide $5,400

The district spends 1 percent of its budget on staff development, as mandated by the state. Fifty percent of this amount is allocated to building initiatives, 25 percent for exemplary programs, and 25 percent to the office of staff development. The Learning Circles/Mentor Program is funded by the office of staff development, and is part of the 25 percent received. In addition, money is obtained from state grants.

Who requests the funding?

Jeanne requests the funding. In addition, she wrote two grants for the 2000–2001 school year, which were funded, that totaled $140,000.

Evaluation of the Program

How is the program evaluated?

Jeanne Klein surveyed the new teachers and the resource colleagues in 1999–2000. She plans to do focus groups in the near future.

Who sees the results?

Jeanne shares the information with the superintendent, other administrators, and the board.

Recruitment, Hiring, and Retention of New Staff

How many new teachers are recruited and hired?

Approximately 300 new teachers are hired each year. Currently 25 percent of the teaching staff is untenured. 40 percent of the teachers are leaving before they are tenured. The average number of years of service is six.

Is there any data that correlates the mentoring program with the retention of new teachers?

Not yet.

What are the indicators of program success?

Reflective comments such as the following indicate the program's success:

> "Although I have taught in other states and am not a 'new teacher,' I found this model very helpful in becoming oriented to St. Paul. Our small group felt comfortable in openly sharing with each other our frustrations, triumphs, and need for help. I especially appreciate my mentor. He consistently went beyond the 'call of duty' to be helpful to us all! Keep the model next year!"

4

Peer Assistance and Review Programs

Columbus Public Schools Peer Assistance and Review Program
Columbus, Ohio

Rochester City School District Career in Teaching Plan
Rochester, New York

COLUMBUS PUBLIC SCHOOLS PEER ASSISTANCE AND REVIEW PROGRAM
COLUMBUS, OHIO

John Grossman, President
Columbus Education Association
929 East Broad Street
Columbus, Ohio 55106
614-253-4731
jgrossman@ceaohio.org
As of July 9, 2001

DEMOGRAPHICS

The following figures are for the 2000-2001 school year.

Grade Levels	K-12 plus specialists	Urban/Suburban/Rural	Urban
Student Population	66,000	Ethnic Makeup* African American Caucasian Hispanic Other	59% 46% 2% 3%
Teacher Population	5,400	% New Teachers	11% (33% of all teachers are in their first three years)
		Per Pupil Expenditure	$7,400

* The statistics available from the district delineated the ethnic makeup as shown.
  There was no information about students of more than one racial heritage.

The following information was obtained from telephone conversations and e-mail correspondence with John Grossman, President of the Columbus Education Association (CEA) as well as materials distributed by the Columbus Education Association.

History

In the mid-1980s, a group of administrators and teachers in the Columbus Schools had researched a number of program designs to

MENTOR PROGRAM

Unique Feature of Program	Peers mentor and evaluate entry-level teachers and experienced teachers in trouble	**Mentoring Is/ Is Not Mandated for Certification/ Licensing**	Is mandated
Cognitive Coaching Is/Is Not a Component	Is a component	**Mentors Do/Do Not Evaluate the New Teachers With Whom They Work**	Do evaluate
Cost of Program	$2,000,000	**Funding**	District and state grants
Mentors Are Full-Time/Part-Time Teachers	Consulting teachers are full-time in that role	**Mentor Remuneration**	Teacher's salary plus 20% of the base
Program in Existence	15 years	**Duration of Program for New Teachers**	1 year; may be longer
Higher Education Affiliation	The Ohio State University	**Program Coordinator**	Coordinated by 7-member panel: 4 union, 3 administrative

assist new teachers. Their hope was to improve retention rates for teachers in urban districts since it was not uncommon for over half of the new teachers to leave within their first year or two, and Columbus was no exception.

Teachers often began in Columbus because of the competitive salaries and access to graduate programs at local colleges, including The Ohio State University (OSU). However, these were not enough to keep them in a challenging urban teaching environment that offered little support in coping with the daily problems they faced as new teachers.

The team of administrators and teachers did a number of site visits to look at induction models. After much deliberation they decided to fashion their program on a model being used in Toledo. It was a similar district, also in Ohio, and it included mentoring and review functions. New teachers would be supported by successful, experienced faculty members, who after a year of observation and reflection, would serve as their primary evaluators. They decided to call the program Peer Assistance and Review (PAR).

State Mandates

Is mentoring mandated for new teachers?
Yes.

Is mentoring part of certification or licensure?
Yes.

Is funding provided to support the mandate?
No. There is some grant money, but it is only available to districts every other year.

Goals

- To retain new teachers
- To put experienced teachers on career ladders, which might offer incentives to them as well as take advantage of the expertise gained by their years of experience

Program Design

What are the components and recommended schedule of the program?
The program includes a variety of professional development experiences for new teachers.

The intern phase is for beginning teachers and involves mentor teachers visiting their classrooms and coaching them.

The other part of the program is the intervention phase; this is for experienced teachers having extreme difficulty. This part of the program does many of the same things as the intern phrase, yet there is not the limit of one year to make a decision about rehiring.

New teacher orientation lasts 1 week with the mentoring component on Thursday and Friday.

Consulting teachers work with new teachers, called interns.

Are there any programs that complement the mentor program?
Yes. Teachers have the option of taking any of three graduate courses offered, including an action research course and a common issues

course. District staff and university faculty jointly teach these courses. They are part of the Virtual University that is in place in the Columbus Public Schools.

Who designed the mentor program?

The program was jointly designed by the school board and the union, 17 years ago.

Program Administration

Who coordinates the mentor program?

The union and the school administration jointly coordinate the program.

Responsibility for the entire management of PAR rests on a seven-member governing panel, referred to as the PAR panel. Members include the union president, three teachers, a personnel executive, the director of contract relations for the district, and a building principal. Chairmanship of the panel rotates between administration and union on a yearly basis. All governing decisions are made by this body, including selection of consulting teachers, monitoring of the consulting teachers' duties and reports, establishment of program policy, and ensuring that the philosophical base for PAR is maintained and refined as necessary.

How is information communicated to shareholders?

Information is communicated through a weekly union newspaper.

Administrative members are responsible for maintaining open lines of communication with the school board and administrative personnel. The union members of the PAR panel seek to keep their faculty representatives and members informed of the purpose and activities of the PAR program as well as advise all members that their legal and contractual rights will be protected whether they are intern teachers in the PAR program or not.

Who coordinates the integration of the mentor program with other professional development opportunities/requirements in the school/ district?

The PAR panel coordinates the integration of the program with other professional development opportunities.

Participants

Who is served?

Entry-level teachers are served by the PAR program, as well as experienced teachers who are having significant difficulties with their practice.

Is participation of new teachers voluntary or mandatory?

Participation of new teachers is mandatory.

Who provides the mentoring/induction?

The Columbus Education Association (CEA), the Columbus Public Schools (CPS), and The Ohio State University (OSU) support the new teachers.

What are the criteria for being a consulting teacher?

The criteria for selection of consulting teachers include

- Five years classroom experience in Columbus
- Outstanding classroom teaching ability
- Talent in written and oral communications
- Ability to work cooperatively and effectively with staff members
- Extensive knowledge of a variety of management and instructional techniques

In addition, each applicant must submit the following documents directly to the manager of personnel:

- A reference from his or her building principal or immediate supervisor
- A reference from his or her union senior faculty representative
- References from two other teachers with whom the applicant is currently working

Each applicant selected for an interview is given a set of questions requiring written responses. These are reviewed for what they reveal about the applicant's attitudes and knowledge, as well as for written communication skills. The applicant then has an extensive oral interview with the panel as the final step in assessing his or her qualifications to be a PAR consulting teacher.

Consulting teachers are expected to be among those most respected by their peers. Because of the importance of their role, in addition to being outstanding teachers, their integrity must be above question. Teachers may serve as consulting teachers for no more than three years before returning to the classroom. Thus no one in the PAR program has been far from the classroom for long. Rather, they are teachers who have sought change and challenge as a way to improve themselves while serving in a vital role for new teachers.

Once selected, potential consulting teachers join a pool of teachers who may be called on to join the PAR program as the need arises. Selections are made as necessary, determined by the number of intern teachers within a particular grade level of content area.

What are the job responsibilities of the consulting teacher?

- Meet with the intern teacher 25 times a year for peer observation and coaching
- Mentor, support, and provide continuous feedback
- Make an assessment of how the teacher is doing and make a recommendation of whether the person should be hired the next year (reviewed by the PAR panel)

Is peer observation and coaching a requirement?

Yes.

Do consulting teachers have full-time classroom teaching responsibilities?

No.

How are consulting teachers available to participate in the program?

Consulting teachers are released from classroom teaching and are full-time supporters of new teachers. They work with 16 to 18 new teachers.

How are consulting teachers selected?

The PAR panel selects the consulting teachers.

Are consulting teachers paid?

Consulting teachers are paid an additional 20 percent of their base salary.

How are matches made between consulting teachers and new teachers?

New teachers are matched with mentors by the subjects and/or ages of students they teach: primary, intermediate, middle, high school.

Are consulting teachers trained?

Consulting teachers are offered a variety of graduate courses, depending on their professional needs and prior education. The PAR panel determines what courses they are required to take. The consulting teachers also participate in workshops every other Friday for the three years they are in the program.

Who supervises consulting teachers?

The PAR panel supervises the consulting teachers.

What supports are available for consulting teachers?

Is there professional development for the consulting teachers?

Consulting teachers receive ongoing staff development. When the program first started, the OSU faculty planned a series of graduate courses for the consulting teachers. These courses were intended to ensure that the participants understood the dynamics of observation and conferencing. They were also aimed at underscoring the importance of a supportive relationship between the intern and the consulting teacher.

Over the years, collaboration with the OSU increased to the point where, in 1998, a part-time position was established for consultation with PAR staff. A professor who had been very involved with the PAR staff development program was given the appointment.

Central to the university's program is the notion that consulting teachers need to look back on their experiences and reflect on how they evolved from beginners to competent professionals. As part of this process they are expected to look at the educational research on the needs and growth of the teachers.

Consulting teachers consider that entry-level teachers progress through a series of stages in their professional development, and that part of the mentoring role is to understand these stages and to help the beginners move from one stage to the next.

Who provides it?

The pre-service training is provided by active PAR consulting teachers.

What resources are available for consulting teachers?

See below.

Do consulting teachers evaluate new teachers?

Yes, consulting teachers evaluate new teachers. This is a central tenet of the Columbus program, and it is contrary to the belief that mentoring and evaluation are conflicting roles. The PAR program assumes that the two functions can be successfully performed by one person. Theoretically, the final evaluation of a beginning teacher would reflect the dialogue that began in September. It wouldn't contain anything new; there would not be any surprises.

Therefore, a lot of attention is given to the need for honesty and candor, as well as support, to be the hallmarks of the relationship between the two teachers. This is a demanding role for consulting teachers and they are carefully chosen for their ability to balance these factors. They are colleagues, not professional evaluators, and their final recommendations stem from their relationships as supportive, consulting teachers.

Is the mentor/new teacher relationship confidential?

Yes, it is confidential.

What are the resources required for the program?

- Salaries for consulting teachers $1,500,000
- New teacher orientation $50,000–70,000
- Salaries for 1 1/2 secretaries   Varies
- Furniture and supplies   Varies
- Materials   Varies

The total cost of the program is approximately $2,000,000.

Funding

In 1986, the school board agreed to fund the million-dollar program. There is sometimes state funding through a grant.

Who requests the funding?

The school board funds the program as a line item in the school budget.

Administrative members of the seven-member panel are responsible for securing necessary financial support of the program.

Evaluation of the Program

How is the program evaluated?
The consulting teachers and new teachers are surveyed.

Who sees the results?
The PAR panel sees the results.

Recruitment, Hiring, and Retention of New Staff

How many new teachers are recruited and hired?
It varies. In 2000–2001, between 500 and 600 teachers were hired, and about as many are anticipated for 2001–2002.

Is there any data that correlates the mentoring program with the retention of new teachers?
Yes. There have been three surveys of staff, assessing the retention rate of teachers after five years in the district. Compared to the 50 percent retention rate cited by Linda Darling-Hammond, the results in Columbus have been much higher:

- In the first five years, 80 percent of the teachers remained, and of the 20 percent who left, 4 to 6 percent of them had been terminated in their first year.
- In the second five-year cycle, 4 to 6 percent terminated, and 81 percent remained.
- In the third five-year cycle, the retention rate dropped to 67 percent.

The union and the district started a research project to determine the reasons for the decline. The preliminary results say that the program has become so accepted in the region, the suburban districts are trying to lure teachers away. Of the teachers who have left, the majority of them have remained in the profession.

What are the indicators of success?
In addition to the retention of new teachers, there are several other indicators of success.

The Columbus Public Schools have worked with Sandra Stroot, at The Ohio State University. She studies when teachers gain competence, and this information helps consulting teachers know how best to help the intern teachers.

Research has been done on the 6,000–7,000 teachers who have participated in the PAR program. Data has been collected about the colleges the teachers had attended, and feedback has been given to the universities of what is working and what needs improvement.

PRAXIS III is teacher testing that is newly mandated, but not yet implemented. All of the PAR consultants have been trained to administer the PRAXIS III test. PAR consultants have deep knowledge of what is required and are incorporating this knowledge into their practice with their intern teachers.

The district has made it clear that the PAR program is the last program that will ever be cut. The explicit due process in the program, as well as all of the data that is collected, addresses the issues of job performance long before any disagreement about tenure would occur. It has put an end to questions of job performance and disputes between the union and the school system.

ROCHESTER CITY SCHOOL DISTRICT CAREER IN TEACHING PLAN
ROCHESTER, NEW YORK

Carl O'Connell, Mentor Program Coordinator
131 West Broad Street
Rochester, New York 14614
716-262-8541
Fax: 651-793-5490
cesmo@aol.com
As of July 9, 2001

DEMOGRAPHICS

The following figures are for the 2000-2001 school year.

Grade Levels	Pre K–Adult Ed	Urban/Suburban/Rural	Urban
Student Population	38,000	Ethnic Makeup* African American Hispanic Caucasian Other	 63% 18% 17% 2%
Teacher Population	3,900	% New Teachers	27%
		Per Pupil Expenditure	$11,000

* The statistics available from the district delineated the ethnic makeup as shown.
There was no information about students of more than one racial heritage.

The following information was obtained from conversations and e-mail correspondence with Adam Urbanski and Carl O'Connell.

History

Adam Urbanski is President of the Rochester Federation of Teachers, and Vice President of the American Federation of Teachers. Through his association with Dal Lawrence, President of the American Federation, Adam became familiar with the Peer Assistance

MENTOR PROGRAM

Unique Feature of Program	Peer assistance and review	Mentoring Is/Is Not Mandated for Certification/Licensing	Is not mandated
Cognitive Coaching Is/Is Not a Component	Is a component	Mentors Do/Do Not Evaluate the New Teachers With Whom They Work	Do evaluate
Cost of Program	$ 4.8 million	Funding	District, state, and grants
Mentors Are Full-Time/Part-Time Teachers	Mentors teach 50% and mentor 50% if they work with 4 new teachers; Otherwise, they are full-time teachers	Mentor Remuneration	Teacher's salary + 5-10% of base
Program in Existence	15 years	Duration of Program for New Teachers	1 year, or longer if requested by teacher or panel
Higher Education Affiliation	None	Program Coordinator	Carl O'Connell

and Review (PAR) program in Toledo, Ohio, which started in 1981. Adam proposed a variation of that program for Rochester in 1986. After multiple meetings, consensus was reached within the Rochester Federation and PAR was proposed in negotiations. It was included in the 1987 contract.

State Mandates

Is mentoring mandated for new teachers?
No.

Is mentoring part of certification or licensure?
No.

Is funding provided to support the mandate?
No. Sometimes the state provides funding.

Goals

- To cultivate good teaching
- To create the best possible teaching staff among the new teachers

Program Design

What are the components and recommended schedule of the program?
The components of the program are:
- Each new teacher is assigned a mentor, who works closely with her/him throughout the school year. New teachers are "interns" on the career level in the Rochester City School District.
- The mentor coaches and evaluates the intern and, at the end of the school year, makes a recommendation to the Career in Teaching panel regarding the teacher's continued employment in the school system.
- There is mentor training before school starts, as well as periodic meetings and training throughout the school year.
- There is a 4-day new teacher orientation the week before school starts.
- There is a Career in Teaching (CIT) panel, composed of teachers and administrators, which reviews the performance of the interns and the mentors.

The panel also arranges training.

Are there any programs that complement the mentor program?
There are career levels as follows:

- Intern—new teachers
- Resident—teachers in their second and third year of teaching
- Professional—tenured teachers
- Lead—teachers who are master teachers and who have additional responsibilities
- There is a UleaD Professional Development group within the union, which collaborates with the CIT department. This group makes recommendations about professional development,

which are often funded by the union and the district. Typically there are 50 professional development opportunities during the school year.

- Tenured teachers may voluntarily request support—peer assistance—which is confidential. In these cases, mentors are assigned to teachers and they work together throughout the school year. No written reports are filed.

Who designed the mentor program?

Initially, Adam Urbanksi designed the program, and then he collaborated with the superintendent, Peter McWalters, and the chair of the CIT panel, Tom Gillett. In 1991, Carl joined the group, and he and school-based mentors also collaborated on design revisions.

Program Administration

Who coordinates the mentor program?

Carl O'Connell is the mentor program coordinator.

How is information communicated to shareholders?

Information is shared through bulletins, articles, and publications about the program. It is also shared at orientation meetings and trainings throughout the school year.

Who coordinates the integration of the mentor program with other professional development opportunities/requirements in the school/district?

The CIT panel works to coordinate the program with other professional development opportunities, and works closely with curriculum directors as well.

Participants

Who is served?

- First-year teachers, newly graduated from college
- Teachers from out of state
- Teachers changing tenure areas
- Uncertified teachers

Is participation of new teachers voluntary or mandatory?

Teachers listed above must participate in the mentor program. Tenured teachers have the option of requesting support.

Who provides the mentoring/induction?

Mentors are classroom teachers. This is a practitioner-based model.

What are the criteria for being a mentor?

- Seven years teaching experience, five in the district
- Tenured
- References from five colleagues, including the supervisor and union representative

What are the job responsibilities of the mentor?

The job responsibilities are those of gatekeeper and evaluator, as well as advocate.

Mentors must:

- Participate in the training, before school and during the school year
- Attend monthly meetings
- Observe and conference with intern(s)
- Do demonstration lessons and peer coach
- Write reports about intern performance
- Recommend whether intern(s) should be rehired

Is peer observation and coaching a requirement for mentors?

Yes, peer observation and coaching is required of mentors. Typically mentors observe 30-40 times and conference with the interns 50-60 times per year.

Do mentors have full-time classroom teaching responsibilities?

All mentors are on the "lead teacher" career level. Mentors who have one intern have full-time classroom teaching responsibilities, and are released on a per diem basis for their mentoring. Mentors who have four interns are released from 50 percent of their teaching.

How are mentors available to participate in the program?

Mentors who have one intern are released on a per diem basis, and substitutes cover their classrooms.

Mentors who are released 50 percent of the time, to mentor four interns, job-share a position. The reaction to this arrangement has been favorable, and parents often request that their children be placed in the classrooms of mentors who are job-sharing.

How are mentors selected?

The CIT panel selects the mentors. Selection is based on:

- Application and statement
- References
- Interview

Are mentors paid?

Mentors are lead teachers, and they are paid an additional 5-10 percent of their base salary, depending on their responsibilities.

How are matches made between mentors and new teachers?

Carl carefully matches interns and mentors. He gives priority to proximity and certification area. It is preferable for interns to be mentored by teachers in their buildings. Yet if those teachers have not taught in their certification area, other mentors are assigned.

Are mentors trained?

Yes, mentors are trained before school starts and then throughout the school year.

Who supervises mentors?

Carl supervises the mentors. In addition, the interns write evaluations of the mentors three times a year, which are reviewed by the CIT panel. Members of the panel share the responsibility for observing each mentor.

What supports are available for mentors?

District personnel support the mentors. They are given materials, including books about beginning teaching, that are also given to interns.

Is there professional development for the mentors?

Yes, there is professional development throughout the school year.

Who provides it?

Professional development is provided by people from within and outside of the system, as the need requires.

What resources are available for mentors?

The monthly meetings are an opportunity for mentors to receive support and discuss issues.

Do mentors evaluate new teachers?

Yes, mentors evaluate their peers. Mentors submit two status reports during the school year, as well as a final report, to the CIT panel. The CIT panel then writes its recommendation about future employment to the superintendent and the Board of Education. In addition, the principal evaluates new teachers.

Is the mentor/new teacher relationship confidential?

Yes, the relationship is confidential. All notes taken by the mentor during observations and conferences with the intern are confidential. The CIT panel is given two status reports and a final evaluation, and the only thing that goes into the new teacher's personnel file is the letter from the CIT panel regarding recommendation for future employment.

What are the resources required for the program?

The total cost of the program is 4.8 million dollars. It costs approximately $4,000 per intern.

The resources required are:

1. Mentor training	$20,000
2. New-teacher orientation	$50,000
3. Books for mentors and interns	$30,000
4. Stipends for mentors	$2,000,000
5. Coverage for mentors to be released	$1,000,000
6. Coordinator and secretary's salaries	$80,000
7. Additional costs:	$1,620,000

- Conferences for interns to attend
- Conferences for mentors to attend
- Supplies and materials
- Copying costs for handbooks

Funding

What are the funding sources?

The funding sources are local, state, and grants.

Who requests the funding?

Carl requests the funding.

Evaluation of the Program

How is the program evaluated?

The program is evaluated throughout the school year in many ways including:

- Mentors' evaluations
- Interns' evaluations
- Administrators' evaluations
- Second-year teachers' survey
- CIT panel observations and review of mentors' records

Who sees the results?

The results of the evaluations are seen by Carl, the union president, and the superintendent.

Recruitment, Hiring, and Retention of New Staff

How many new teachers are recruited and hired?

700 new teachers were hired in the 2000–2001 school year.

Is there any data that correlates the mentoring program with the retention of new teachers?

Yes. In 1986, before the program was started, 65 percent of new teachers remained in the district. The first year of the program, 1987, the retention rate grew to 91 percent. Over the last 15 years, the average retention rate is 86.6 percent.

What are the indicators of program success?

In addition to the retention rate, there are other indicators of success, including:

- Information regarding how well the students of intern teachers did on the English Language Arts (ELA) test given to all fourth graders, as compared with the students of tenured teachers.
- The Education Testing and Research Department in the Rochester City School District concluded, "In short, the ELA longitudinal study offered tantalizing evidence that the mentor program is an effective intervention in improving student performance."

5

State-Funded Programs

Beginning Teacher Program
Joint School District No. 2
Meridian, Idaho

Muscogee County School District Teacher Mentoring Program
Columbus, Georgia

Beginning Educator Support and Training Program
North Haven Public Schools
North Haven, Connecticut

Beginner Teacher Support and Assessment Program
Pajaro Valley Unified School District
Watsonville, California

Lee County Schools Model New Teacher Mentoring Program
Sanford, North Carolina

BEGINNING TEACHER PROGRAM, JOINT SCHOOL DISTRICT NO. 2 MERIDIAN, IDAHO

Mark VanSkiver, Director
1760 West Pine Street
Meridian, Idaho 83642
208-888-6701
Fax: 208-288-1093
vanskiver@meridianschools.org
As of July 9, 2001

DEMOGRAPHICS

The following figures are for the 2000-2001 school year.

Grade Levels	K-12	Urban/Suburban/Rural	This joint district has urban, suburban, and rural school systems
Student Population	24,000	Ethnic Makeup*	
Teacher Population	1,500	% New Teachers	8% (33% of teachers are in their first three years)
		Per Pupil Expenditure	$4,600

* No information available.

The following information was obtained from interviews with Mark VanSkiver, Administrator of Instructional Support Services, and Brenda Mahler, beginning teacher advisor, and quoted from written materials printed by Joint School District No. 2.

State Mandates

Is mentoring mandated for new teachers?

Yes, beginning in September of 2001, it was mandated that a mentor program be provided for teachers in their first three years of their contract.

MENTOR PROGRAM

Unique Feature of Program	A 3-year program with full- and part-time mentors	Mentoring Is/ Is Not Mandated for Certification/ Licensing	Is mandated
Cognitive Coaching Is/ Is Not a Component	Is a component	Mentors Do/Do Not Evaluate the New Teachers With Whom They Work	Do not evaluate
Cost of Program	$325,000	Funding	State appropriates $512/new teacher; local covers rest
Mentors Are Full-Time/ Part-Time Teachers	Full-time beginning teacher advisors; Part-time building mentors	Mentor Remuneration	Building mentors: $200; Beginning teacher advisors: Teacher's salary plus 10 extra days
Program in Existence	3 years	Duration of Program for New Teachers	3 years
Higher Education Affiliation	None	Program Coordinator	Mark VanSkiver, Instructional Support Services

Is mentoring part of certification or licensure?

Yes.

Is funding provided to support the mandate?

Yes, the State gives the district $512 a year for teachers in their first three years.

Goals

The goal of the program is to provide new teachers with profes-sional support to ensure their successful induction into the teaching profession. Joint School District No. 2 is committed to providing every student with a teacher of integrity, possessing the interpersonal and technical skills to promote high quality instruction. Through the implementation of the Beginning Teacher Program, beginning teachers in Joint School District No. 2 have greater opportunity to develop the following competencies:

- Engage and support all students in learning
- Create and maintain effective learning environments for student achievement
- Plan and organize comprehensive curriculum for student learning
- Design and implement teaching strategies to meet the needs of diverse learners
- Assess and report student achievement through a variety of traditional and authentic measures
- Communicate effectively with parents and patrons
- Collaborate effectively with education professionals

Program Design

What are the components and recommended schedule of the Beginning Teacher Program and the mentor program?

The components of the Beginning Teacher Program include:

- An orientation
- Six beginning teacher advisors, who work full time to support each new teacher in the system
- Monthly workshops
- An orientation conference
- Informal conferencing
- Formal/informal observations (in a cognitive coaching model)
- Demonstration lessons
- Mid-year goal setting
- End-of-year summary conference
- Professional growth portfolios
- Beginning Teacher Seminar (optional)

The components of the mentor program for teachers in their first three years include:

- An orientation
- A building mentor for each teacher

- Informal conferencing
- Peer assistance program, which provides additional help on request, from curriculum coordinators and staff developers

Are there any programs that complement the mentor program?

There is a Teacher Academy that provides extensive professional development in the school district. The Academy offers a variety of coursework, and teachers can receive credit from either of three local universities. The school system underwrites 50–60 percent of the cost of the courses.

Teachers in their first three years in the district must complete twelve credits in order to move to Level 2 of the salary scale. Six of those credits are required, and they specifically relate to programs in the district. They include training in the continuous improvement initiative, concept-based curriculum, assessment of student learning, comprehensive literacy, and behavior management.

The Beginning Teacher Seminar is an optional course and the tuition is paid by the school system for teachers who take it.

Who designed the mentor program?

Mark VanSkiver, Administrator of Instructional Support Services, and a mentor committee composed of building principals, central office administrators, and teachers designed the program.

Program Administration

Who coordinates the program?

Mark coordinates the program.

How is information communicated to shareholders?

Mark communicates with the school board and districts throughout the state that are replicating the model. Mark shares evaluation feedback from new teachers with respondents to the survey, as well as writing it up in an annual report to the board and the administrators.

Who coordinates the integration of this program with other professional development opportunities/requirements in the school/district?

Mark coordinates the integration of this program with other professional development opportunities.

Participants

Who is served?

The Beginning Teacher Program is for teachers in their first year in the profession. The mentor program is for teachers in their first three years in the district.

Is participation of new teachers voluntary or mandatory?

First-year teachers must participate in the Beginning Teacher Program.

The district is mandated by the state to provide a mentor program for teachers in their first three years in the system. The building principal orients new staff and explains all the supports available, and assigns a building mentor to all teachers in their first three years of employment. The second and third year teachers may opt to waive other services that support their induction, and they do so by signing off on those other supports.

Who provides the mentoring/induction?

There are six beginning teacher advisors who work with teachers new to the profession and who are in their first year in the system.

Building mentors are assigned to all teachers in their first, second, and third year in the system.

What are the criteria for being a teacher advisor?

The selection of beginning teacher advisors is based on the following professional competencies:

- Demonstrated outstanding professional teaching ability
- Demonstrated extensive knowledge in a variety of classroom management and instructional techniques
- Demonstrated professional knowledge of student assessment
- Demonstrated skillful written and oral communication
- Demonstrated leadership ability and commitment to the teaching profession
- Demonstrated ability to work collaboratively with professional staff

What are the job responsibilities of the beginning teacher advisors?

- Meet frequently with assigned beginning teachers
- Provide emotional support and encouragement
- Provide coaching

- Help with curriculum, assessment, and instructional planning
- Demonstrate effective teaching practices
- Provide guidance and strategies for student behavior management
- Collaborate with beginning teachers to write self-reflective performance summaries
- Guide goal setting process
- Provide oral and written feedback on progress toward goals
- Offer advice and support for parent communication
- Be a resource for understanding school district policies and procedures
- Arrange for beginning teachers to visit master teacher classrooms
- Act as contact for resource personnel

Beginning teacher advisors each work with between 18 and 20 new teachers.

Building mentors are guides on the side. They provide general assistance in the building and may informally coach or advise. Since new teachers in their first year also work closely with beginning teacher advisors who do cognitive coaching with them, the mentors do not typically do the coaching process in its entirety.

Is peer observation and coaching a requirement for the mentor?

All beginning teacher advisors are trained in cognitive coaching. This is a nonevaluative process that promotes pre- and post-observation reflection by the new teacher. Though a minimum of four coaching cycles are encouraged, they are not required. Many new teachers choose to do cognitive coaching with their beginning teacher advisor even more than four times during the school year.

Beginning teacher advisors minimally meet with each new teacher every ten days; however, they usually meet with them weekly for one to two hours.

Do beginning teacher advisors have full-time classroom teaching responsibilities?

No, they work full time to support the teachers who are in their first year in the profession.

How are beginning teacher advisors/mentors selected?

Mark, central office personnel, and other advisors interview applicants. Strong recommendations from principals and the candidates' peers are required.

Mentors are selected by their building principals. The criteria for their selection includes three years teaching experience in the profession and excellent instructional and interpersonal skills.

What is the salary for beginning teacher advisors/mentors?

Beginning teacher advisors have a teacher salary contract, and their contract is extended by ten additional days.

Mentors are paid $200 a year.

How are matches made between beginning teacher advisors and new teachers?

The beginning teacher advisors work in either the secondary schools or the elementary schools. At the secondary level, it is not necessary for the advisors to specialize in the same subjects as the new teachers, because advisors will arrange for help from subject-specific teachers to work with new teachers as well. Beginning teacher advisors work in regions, and support all the first-year teachers who are new to the profession. One advisor works in the traditional elementary schools and another one works in the year-round elementary schools.

Are beginning teacher advisors trained?

Beginning teacher advisors receive five days of extensive training in cognitive coaching, building trust and rapport, developing interpersonal skills, and the framework of the program and tools for implementing it successfully.

Mark originally gave the training; now experienced beginning teacher advisors train new advisors. Cognitive coaching is taught by a regional trainer.

Who supervises beginning teacher advisors and mentors?

Mark supervises beginning teacher advisors. Building principals supervise the mentors.

What supports are available for beginning teacher advisors?

Is there professional development for beginning teacher advisors?

There is ongoing training for beginning teacher advisors.

Who provides it?

Any training that is planned for teachers is also offered to beginning teacher advisors, as well as updates and other training they request.

What resources are available for beginning teacher advisors?

The resources available to beginning teacher advisors include district resources, conferencing with school personnel, and other materials they request.

Do beginning teacher advisors evaluate new teachers?

No, beginning teacher advisors do not evaluate teachers. Principals evaluate teachers.

Is the relationship between the beginning teacher advisor and the new teacher confidential?

Yes, the relationship is totally confidential.

What are the resources required for the program?

- Salary for beginning teacher advisors $250,000
- Building mentors' stipend $20,000
- Substitutes $40,000
- Travel reimbursement $6,000
- Supplies $5,000
- Professional development
  (travel) for advisors $4,000

This year the state gave $257,000, and the district gave $68,000.

Who requests the funding?

The state calculates the funding based on the number of new teachers in the district. The remainder of the money comes from the district budget, at the project director's request.

Evaluation of the Program

How is the program evaluated?

New teachers complete mid- and end-of-the-year surveys.

Who sees the results?

The surveys are returned to Mark's office, where they are tabulated. Then they are shared with the respondents and the school board. The feedback from the surveys is used to improve the program.

Recruitment, Hiring, and Retention of New Staff

How many new teachers are recruited and hired?

In the 2000–2001 school year, there were 118 teachers in their first year.

Is there any data that correlates the mentoring program with the retention of new teachers?

Not yet.

What are the indicators of program success?

The growth of the program is a major indicator of success. Building principals find the program invaluable. They know that their first-year teachers are getting supported in ways that principals would not be able to provide because of multiple demands on the principals' time. The principals insisted that the program continue and be expanded. The data from the surveys of new teachers show really strong support of the program.

MUSCOGEE COUNTY SCHOOL DISTRICT TEACHER MENTORING PROGRAM
COLUMBUS, GEORGIA

Louise Tolbert, System Mentor Coordinator
Claflin Instructional Center
1532 Fifth Avenue
Columbus, Georgia 31901-1996
706-649-0588
Fax: 706-641-4160
ljtolbert@mindspring.com
As of July 9, 2001

DEMOGRAPHICS

The following figures are for the 2000-2001 school year.

Grade Levels	Pre K-12	Urban/Suburban/Rural	Urban and suburban
Student Population	33,000	**Ethnic Makeup** African American Asian American Caucasian Hispanic Multiracial Native American	 60.2% 1.3% 33.8% 2.8% 1.7% 0.2%
Teacher Population	3,000	**% New Teachers**	10%
		Per Pupil Expenditure	$5,642

The following information was obtained from telephone conversations and e-mail correspondence with Louise Tolbert.

History

There was a mentoring program ten years ago. Mentors weren't paid at that time. The state offered a Teacher Support Specialist (TSS) program and the mentoring program in Muscogee County was changed to the present model.

MENTOR PROGRAM

Unique Feature of Program	Best Practices workshops offered after school throughout the year	Mentoring Is/ Is Not Mandated for Certification/ Licensing	Is not mandated
Cognitive Coaching Is/ Is Not a Component	Is a component	Mentors Do/Do Not Evaluate the New Teachers With Whom They Work	Do not evaluate
Cost of Program	$312,300	Funding	State supports much of it, some local contributions
Mentors Are Full-Time/Part-Time Teachers	Full-time	Mentor Remuneration	Paid per unit (15 hours of mentoring) based on funds allocated by state
Program in Existence	10 years	Duration of Program for New Teachers	3 years
Higher Education Affiliation	Columbus State University	Program Coordinator	Louise Tolbert

State Mandates

Is mentoring mandated for new teachers?

No.

Is mentoring part of certification or licensure?

No.

Is funding provided to support the mandate?

Yes. Funds are available for classroom teachers who are trained as mentors and who mentor new teachers. There is a specific amount of money allocated, and it is divided among the teachers in the state who submit requests for the stipend. This year,1.4 million dollars was allocated for this purpose.

Goals

The mission of the Muscogee County School District mentoring program is to provide eligible teachers with a nurturing environment, necessary resources, and guidance to develop and apply strategies that will ensure a rewarding, effective teaching career.

Program Design

What are the components and recommended schedule of the program?

- New teachers are assigned a mentor.
- There are 4 system mentors, including the elementary, middle, and high school levels, as well as the director who supports the elementary teachers. The system mentors for the 2000–2001 school year were Penny Thornton, Tina Jones, and Jo Gilliland.
- New teachers are given the *New Teacher Handbook*.
- There is a two-day, new teacher orientation in the fall, which includes meetings with mentors, introductions to central office administrators, and encouragement from the system's cheer-leading team.
- There are approximately 25 Best Practices workshops after school, throughout the school year. New teachers must attend a minimum of five of these workshops, though many attend more. The workshops are also open to other teachers. Some of the topics include: dealing with tragedy; how to use technology for easier lesson planning; parent conferencing; alternative assessment; student-centered learning.
- There is an Idea Fair in February. It is a festive afterschool event, with decorations and eye-catching displays that entice viewers to visit displays of best practices set up by teachers. This has become very popular, with 300 teachers in attendance. In addition to new teachers, veteran teachers, and even teachers from other districts attend this event. A mini-Idea Fair is part of the new teacher orientation in the fall.
- Periodically workshops are offered.
- There are three years of induction.

Are there any programs that complement the mentor program?
No.

Who designed the mentor program?
Louise Tolbert designed the program.

Program Administration

Who coordinates the program?
Louise Tolbert coordinates the program.

How is information communicated to shareholders?
Louise is in close contact with the principals, both at meetings and through written correspondence. She developed an end-of-the-year evaluation form that principals will complete.

Who coordinates the integration of this program with other professional development opportunities/requirements in the school/district?
Efforts are made by program directors to coordinate the professional development opportunities in the district.

Participants

Who is served?
Teachers in their first three years participate in the program. Sometimes a teacher may extend participation for a fourth year to gain additional competence.

Is participation of new teachers voluntary or mandatory?
Participation in this three-year program is mandatory.

Who provides the mentoring/induction?
See below.

What are the criteria for being a mentor?
The criteria for being a mentor are:

- At least three years of teaching experience in the district
- A valid teaching certificate
- Evidence of excellent interpersonal skills

- Demonstrated professional competence
- Willingness to commit the additional time necessary for support responsibilities

After the management teams have approved mentor candidates, an application with two recommendations is submitted to Louise. Louise and other system mentors observe the mentor candidates in their classrooms to finalize their selections.

What are the job responsibilities of the mentor?

Mentors support their new-teacher partners in many ways, including:

- Giving a tour of the school
- Introducing them to new colleagues and helping build relationships
- Helping set up classrooms (which may include finding materials)
- Providing day-to-day support
- Doing observations and conferencing once each quarter
- Completing documentation of meetings and conferences
- Sharing lesson plans
- Advocating if there is a problem

Lead Teacher Support Specialists hold meetings with new teachers every 6 weeks. They are building contacts for system mentors.

System mentors in middle and high school work with the director (who works in the elementary schools) to:

- Support mentors and new teachers
- Do model lessons
- Prepare *Lifesavers,* a monthly newsletter for new teachers
- Prepare newsletters for Teacher Support Specialists each month
- Meet with administrators and teachers when there are concerns about job performance
- Provide feedback and support for teachers having difficulty performing their responsibilities
- Collaborate on the implementation of the mentoring program

Is peer observation and coaching a requirement for the mentor?

Yes, peer observation and coaching is a requirement of mentoring.

Do mentors have full-time classroom teaching responsibilities?

Yes, mentors are full-time teachers.

How are mentors available to participate in the program?

Mentor training is done in the summer, or after school hours.

Mentors meet with new teachers during common preparation periods, lunchtimes, and after school hours.

How are mentors selected?

Principals recommend teachers as mentors to the management team in their buildings, which is composed of teachers, other staff, and often parents. The management team seeks the following criteria:

- Demonstrates outstanding instructional skill
- Demonstrates effective classroom management skill
- Conveys verbally and nonverbally an enthusiasm for teaching
- Models professional and ethical attitudes and behaviors
- Shows genuine interest in helping other teachers and a willingness to spend the time required
- Is willing to listen, be tolerant, and to convey empathy
- Has the ability to be secure, sensitive, flexible, and caring while working with others
- Is energetic, enthusiastic, and positive toward others
- Is able to clearly and effectively communicate thoughts and knowledge about teaching practices to others
- Seeks and accepts a leadership role and other responsibilities in the school

Are mentors paid?

Yes, mentors are paid by the state, according to the number of units they mentor. Each unit is 15 hours of mentoring, which is the minimum requirement per quarter. Mentors submit to the state the number of units they worked, and the state-allocated money is divided among the mentors requesting stipends. Sometimes each unit is worth $150–$250. Typically mentors receive $500 or less for the year.

The system mentors work 11 months a year, and receive a prorated teacher's salary.

The director works 12 months a year, also on a teacher's salary contract.

How are matches made between mentors and new teachers?

Principals match mentors and new teachers, sometimes with the help of the system mentors. They consider grade or subject taught, and make an effort to match for mutual planning periods.

Are mentors trained?

Yes, mentors participate in 100 hours of training. The first 50 hours are courses, offered after school or in the summer. Some of the things they learn are the needs of new teachers, the role of the mentor, conferencing skills, and effective teaching techniques.

The next 50 hours are called internships, during which the mentor works with teachers in their first three years of teaching. After mentors log in 40 hours, they attend 10 more hours of classes, at which they discuss the mentoring process and revisit materials and best practices. Colleagues, who were trained by the state, train mentors.

Who supervises mentors?

Louise supervises mentors.

What supports are available for mentors?

Is there professional development for the mentors?

Workshops are offered throughout the year. Mentors are often invited first, and then other teachers and specialists are also invited to attend. Topics have included textbook adoption, testing, Ames mathematics and science, Marilyn Burns's mathematics materials, and time management.

Who provides it?

Workshops are offered by colleagues, as well as presenters from outside the system.

What resources are available for mentors?

- Teacher resource room
- Production room, with magazines, books, and materials
- Professional library for Teacher Support Specialists
- A bound collection of the handouts from the Idea Fair is given to each mentor.
- Mentors and new teachers are invited to a dinner celebration at the end of the school year.
- Lead Teacher Support Specialists are given agenda ideas (from system mentors) for their meetings with new teachers.

Do mentors evaluate new teachers?

No, mentors do not evaluate teachers.

Is the mentor-new teacher relationship confidential?

Yes, the relationship is confidential.

On occasion, administrators may meet with a system mentor regarding a concern about a new teacher's job performance. The principal may write a growth plan for the new teacher, which includes the requirement that the new teacher work even more closely with her/his mentor and/or system mentor.

What are the resources required for the program?

For 2001–2002:

- Salaries for system-level mentors: 4 people $227,000
- Mentor training—instructor and materials $1,850
- Benefits $59,700
- Best Practices workshop instructors $5,600
- 3 management courses, each offered
  3 times a year $4,950
- Stipends for mentors
  (these come from the state department)   Varies
- Substitutes for released time $1,900
- In-system travel $1,000
- Out-of-system travel, workshops $5,000
- Supplies $2,300
- Brochure titled *Master Teacher* $1,000
- Printing $2,000
- Hardware and audiovisual equipment (paid
  for by the staff development department) $312,300

Funding

What are the funding sources?

The state provides funds to every district for staff development. In addition, a small grant from the NEA Federal Credit Union helps support this program.

Who requests the funding?

Louise requests funding for the program.

Evaluation of the Program

How is the program evaluated?

The program is evaluated through end-of-the-year surveys of new teachers and course evaluations. A survey for principals has been designed for use this year.

Who sees the results?

Louise and the system mentors see the results and use them for program review and revision.

Recruitment, Hiring, and Retention of New Staff

How many new teachers are recruited and hired?

Approximately 300 new teachers are hired each year.

Is there any data that correlates the mentoring program with the retention of new teachers?

No, there isn't any hard data about retention. In reports to the state about why teachers leave the district, exit interviews have indicated that most of the teachers who are leaving do so because of a spouse's job transfer or child bearing and rearing.

What are the indicators of program success?

- Teacher retention
- Teacher improvement
- Positive relationships between new teachers, mentors, and system mentors
- Surveys and evaluations at the end of the year that reflect the high value of the program
- High ratings on the Best Practices workshops, the Idea Fair, and the new teacher orientation

BEGINNING EDUCATOR SUPPORT AND TRAINING PROGRAM, NORTH HAVEN PUBLIC SCHOOLS NORTH HAVEN, CONNECTICUT

Marie Diamond, BEST Facilitator and Director of Curriculum and Staff Development
5 Linsley Street
North Haven, Connecticut 06473
203-239-2581, x237
diamond.marie@north-haven.k12.ct.us
As of July 9, 2001

DEMOGRAPHICS

The following figures are for the 2000-2001 school year.

Grade Levels	Pre K-12	Urban/Suburban/Rural	This joint district has urban, suburban, and rural school systems
Student Population	3,486	**Ethnic Makeup*** African American American Indian Asian American Caucasian Hispanic	 2.5% 0.03% 3.8% 92.1% 1.2%
Teacher Population	304	**% New Teachers**	11%
		Per Pupil Expenditure Elementary and middle school students High school students	 $6,753 $8,338

* The statistics available from the district delineated the ethnic makeup as shown. There was no information about students of more than one racial heritage.

Excerpts from "A Guide to the BEST Program for Beginning Teachers," published for 2000–2001 by the Connecticut State Department of Education, Bureau of Program and Teacher Evaluation, are included in the following description of the North Haven Public Schools program, along with information obtained from Marie Diamond, the coordinator of the program in North Haven, in telephone conversations and e-mail correspondence.

MENTOR PROGRAM

Unique Feature of Program	This program is part of the state's BEST program	Mentoring Is/ Is Not Mandated for Certification/ Licensing	Is mandated
Cognitive Coaching Is/ Is Not a Component	Is a component	Mentors Do/Do Not Evaluate the New Teachers With Whom They Work	Do not evaluate
Cost of Program	$8,420	Funding	District and state, which gives $200 per new teacher to the district
Mentors Are Full-Time/Part-Time Teachers	Full-time	Mentor Remuneration	$200 per year
Program in Existence	11 years	Duration of Program for New Teachers	2 years; 3 if needed
Higher Education Affiliation		Program Coordinator	Marie Diamond

History

The Education Enhancement Act of 1986 was highly successful in raising standards for teacher education and licensing as well as increasing teacher salaries to the highest in the nation. This "balanced equation" of higher teacher salaries matched by increased professional standards has been extremely successful in attracting more academically qualified individuals into Connecticut's schools.

Connecticut's Common Core of Teaching (CCT) defines the knowledge, skills, and competencies that teachers need to attain in order to ensure that students learn and perform at high levels. The CCT is used across the career continuum of teachers. The CCT includes foundational skills and competencies that are common to all teachers and discipline specific professional standards that represent the knowledge, skills, and competencies that are unique for teachers of elementary education, English language arts, history/social studies, mathematics, music, physical education, science, special education, visual arts and world languages.

The centerpiece of Connecticut's teacher improvement initiatives has been the Beginning Educator Support and Training (BEST) program, a comprehensive three-year induction program for teachers once they are hired in Connecticut public schools.

The North Haven Public School District was motivated to improve its offerings to new teachers, who had always been assigned buddies. When the state introduced BEST, the district was ready to do more.

State Mandates

Is mentoring mandated for new teachers?

Yes, for new teachers for whom there is a BEST program. There is no BEST program for teachers in technology education and some of the other specialties.

Is mentoring part of certification or licensure?

Yes. The BEST program is a comprehensive induction program of support and assessment for beginning teachers. Beginning teachers must successfully complete BEST program requirements in order to be eligible for the provisional educator certificate.

Is funding provided to support the mandate?

Yes. Initially there had been more funding for induction, including stipends for mentors. Now the state reimburses towns $200 for each new teacher registered in BEST.

Goals

The mission of the BEST program is to ensure that every Connecticut student is taught by a highly qualified and competent teacher. The BEST program helps ensure that all beginning teachers have opportunities to strengthen their knowledge of subject matter and instructional strategies, enhance their understanding of students as learners, and begin a process of lifelong learning and professional growth.

Program Design

What are the components and recommended schedule of the program?

Minimum levels of school-based support required through the BEST program in the first year are:

- Assignment of a mentor or support team within ten days of commencing teaching
- Regular contacts with the mentor or support team members (at least biweekly meetings)
- Local district provision of at least eight half-days to observe or be observed by their mentors or support team members for professional-development-related activities
- The equivalent of 30 hours of "significant contacts" over the course of the school year between a beginning teacher and his or her mentor, support team members, content colleagues, the principal and/or district facilitator.

These "significant contacts" may include districtwide BEST orientation meetings, afterschool professional development activities provided by district facilitators, regular meetings such as breakfasts for beginning teachers with the principal, activities introducing beginning teachers to the community, and regularly scheduled staff meetings in which beginning teachers participate.

In the second year, the district may provide mentor or support team assistance. This is at the discretion of the district or school.

Are there any programs that complement the mentor program?

There are state-based support sessions in the first year that include:

- BEST orientation sessions
- Discipline-specific seminars

The central focus of BEST program professional development offerings for beginning teachers is to provide meaningful learning experiences that enable beginning teachers continuously to raise their expectations for their students' achievement and for their teaching. In addition, these sessions provide practical strategies to enhance the capabilities of beginning teachers to increase student learning.

There are state-based support sessions in the second year that include:

- Portfolio overview sessions
- Portfolio videotape sessions
- Discipline-specific seminars

There is a portfolio requirement, in which submission of a teaching portfolio is required by May 1 (April 15 for special education beginning teachers) of the teacher's second year.

Who designed the mentor program?

The BEST program was designed by the State Department of Education. Every school superintendent must appoint a district BEST facilitator, who coordinates and oversees the program. The district facilitator goes to three or four meetings a year, and is updated by the state on the BEST program. The state sets BEST guidelines and requirements, and the BEST district facilitators find ways to address them and support the new teachers in their system. Marie Diamond is the North Haven Public Schools BEST facilitator.

Program Administration

Who coordinates the program?

Marie Diamond coordinates the program in North Haven.

How is information communicated to shareholders?

The Bureau of Program and Teacher Evaluation publishes many documents that are distributed to all beginning teachers, as well as other school personnel. In addition, the district BEST facilitator disseminates relevant materials about the district and state programs.

Who coordinates the integration of this program with other professional development opportunities/requirements in the school/district?

Marie Diamond is the director of curriculum and staff development in the North Haven Public Schools, as well as being the BEST facilitator. Often people in similar positions are the BEST facilitators, and are thereby well positioned to coordinate the integration of the BEST program and the district's induction program with other professional development.

Participants

Who is served?

Teachers who must participate in the BEST program are "beginning" teachers who:

- Are employed as teachers in Connecticut's public school or an approved private special education facility
- Hold one of the following certificates:

  1. Initial educator certificate
  2. Interim initial educator certificate
  3. Temporary 90-day certificate
  4. Durational shortage area permit

- Are full-time or part-time
- Are hired under a long-term substitute status (provided they are teaching under a valid certificate as noted above and in the corresponding endorsement area of that certificate)

The BEST program does not stipulate any support for teachers who change grade levels or subjects; districts may provide assistance. In some cases, teachers are permitted to submit their required portfolio in their third year because of changing subjects.

Is participation of new teachers voluntary or mandatory?

Participation is mandatory. BEST is a two-year program, with a third year available if necessary. However, the third year is the last opportunity to complete the BEST program requirements. Individuals who fail to complete participation in three years will not be eligible for reissuance of the initial educator certificate.

Who provides the mentoring/induction?

Experienced North Haven Public Schools teachers who are trained by the state as BEST support teachers provide the induction support as mentors.

In addition, there are support teams, led by a school staff member who has completed BEST support team training. A support team may support one or more beginning teachers at the district or building level. Other members of the team may include teachers in the same content areas or grade level as the beginning teacher, a previously trained Common Core of Teaching assessor or BEST portfolio scorer, the principal, a department chair, a curriculum specialist, and past "graduates" of the BEST program.

What are the criteria for being a mentor?

The guidelines for the district selection of support teachers (mentors and cooperating teachers) define eligible educators as teachers holding a professional or a provisional education certificate and who have attained tenure.

Qualifications

- Demonstration of success as an educator
- Possession of a variety of educational experiences and training
- Ability to impart knowledge and understanding about effective teaching practices to others
- Demonstrated knowledge of effective teaching practices as defined by the CCT or its equivalent
- Commitment to improving the induction of student and beginning teachers into the profession
- Ability to relate to adult learners and work cooperatively as part of a team
- Demonstration of effective communication skills

What are the job responsibilities of the mentor/support team?

Regardless of whether support is provided by a mentor or a support team, the mentor, or support team, is responsible for assisting the beginning teacher in:

- Exploring a variety of teaching strategies that address diversity in students and their learning styles
- Identifying the effective teaching strategies that conform to the foundational skills and competencies as well as discipline-specific standards of the CCT
- Reflecting on the effectiveness of teaching and how well students are learning
- Documenting the types and frequency of support provided to the beginning teacher

The professional responsibilities of mentors and support teams are:

- To meet regularly (at a minimum, once every two weeks) with the beginning teachers
- To provide instructional support through such activities as observing the beginning teacher's teaching (either in person or through videotape), discussing lesson planning and analyzing student work
- To assist the beginning teacher in demonstrating effective teaching as defined by Connecticut's Common Core of Teaching and in preparing for the BEST portfolio assessment
- To help secure the appropriate resources (e.g., equipment, video camera operation) for beginning teachers to videotape their classrooms for the portfolio assessment as well as for general professional development
- To identify and engage other instructional staff (as needed) in providing the beginning teacher with instructional support in his/her content area and/or grade level.
- To participate in professional development activities related to supporting beginning teachers and enhancing one's own professional practices
- To seek information from the BEST program district facilitator regarding district policies for using professional development funds (funds provided to school districts by the state to support beginning teachers and their mentors)

Is peer observation and coaching a requirement for the mentor?

Yes. Mentors and other support team members may either observe a beginning teacher or view a videotape of teaching to provide feedback about the following critical questions:

- How well were the lesson elements tied together so that students could see a connection between lesson elements, as well as past and future learning?
- How well were lessons developed to move students toward achieving objectives?
- What were the teacher's and the students' roles in classroom discourse?
- How effectively did the teacher monitor understanding and make adjustments as appropriate?

A component of the BEST program that has since been changed was that there were assessors who were trained by the state to observe and evaluate beginning teachers. That has been replaced by the requirement of a portfolio, which is submitted in the teachers' second year. Now the state trains people to assess the portfolios over the summer.

Do mentors have full-time classroom teaching responsibilities?

Yes, mentors are full-time classroom teachers.

How are mentors available to participate in the program?

The BEST program requires that districts provide new teachers with at least eight half-days to observe or be observed by their mentors or support teams or for professional-development-related activities. The difficulty districts face is in finding the substitute teachers needed to fulfill their requirement. Sometimes the district finds other ways to cover classrooms for the observations to occur.

How are mentors selected?

There is an application and informal interview process for prospective support teachers. In addition to inviting applications, Marie asks administrators to recommend teachers to her. Then Marie sends the individual teachers letters, telling them that they have been nominated to be a support teacher and urging them to consider applying.

The selection process includes informal meetings between the candidates and a BEST committee; names are then submitted to the Superintendent of Schools and then the Board of Education for final approval.

Are mentors paid?

State funding no longer includes stipends for support teachers. Districts are given $200 per teacher registered in the BEST program, and Marie has allocated this money for mentor stipends.

How are matches made between mentors and new teachers?

Marie reviews the need for mentors and the mentors who are to be trained. Marie does an annual training of new mentors; however, this is often done before all the needs for mentors are known. Whenever possible, Marie tries to match beginning teachers with mentors who have taught at the same grade or subject level. If teaching experience is not directly matched, Marie works to ensure that teachers have a mentor in their building. Support teams are a way to give beginning teachers support with someone who has expertise in their subject areas, since every person on the support team is not required to have training by the state.

Are mentors trained?

Support teachers, who may also mentor teachers who work with student teachers, are trained by the state. They participate in professional development that includes mentor update training, district support team orientation, and other workshops.

Who supervises mentors?

As district facilitator, Marie oversees the program. She speaks with mentors to get their assurances that they have met the requirements of the program. Marie also meets periodically with the mentors to provide program updates, and to discuss any questions or concerns the mentors have.

What supports are available for mentors?

Marie is available to work with mentors and support teams, as well as their beginning teacher partners.

Is there professional development for the mentors?

There are periodic mentor update workshops offered by the state and the district.

Who provides it?

The Department of Education offers training for the mentors.

What resources are available for mentors?

Mentors have access to audiovisual equipment, as well as support from the district service center.

Do mentors evaluate new teachers?

Mentors do not evaluate beginning teachers. They are providing support to new teachers.

Is the mentor/new teacher relationship confidential?

Mentors, as coaches, are in nonevaluative positions and should not be communicating any concerns to anyone, except if there was a breach of a code of ethics or concerns about the safety of the students.

What are the resources required for the program?

- First-day orientation expenses $550
- Materials for new teachers $820
- Stipends for mentors $6,400
- Video camera $650

Funding

The state provides the district with $200 per beginning trainer registered in the BEST program.

Who requests the funding?

There is a state database of the new teachers in each district.

Further support of the program in North Haven comes from the professional development budget of the district.

Evaluation of the Program

How is the program evaluated?

The state does extensive evaluation of the BEST program, through feedback from teachers and analysis of data regarding student achievement and teacher performance. Some people think that the portfolio is very difficult to do, and that there is not enough support from the state. Mentors are spending a lot of time with the new teachers, and the state is no longer compensating the mentors for their time.

Who sees the results?

Marie periodically speaks with district administrators. State officials see the results of the evaluations.

Recruitment, Hiring, and Retention of New Staff

How many new teachers are recruited and hired?

34 new teachers were hired in the 2000–2001 school year.

Is there any data that correlates the mentoring program with the retention of new teachers?

No.

What are the indicators of program success?

- 100% of the new teachers passed the BEST portfolio requirement for certification
- The new teachers who left the system did so only for larger salary elsewhere or for family relocation reasons
- New teachers, mentors, and administrators responded positively

BEGINNING TEACHER SUPPORT AND ASSESSMENT PROGRAM, PAJARO VALLEY UNIFIED SCHOOL DISTRICT WATSONVILLE, CALIFORNIA

Ellen Moir, Executive Director
New Teacher Center, University of California, Santa Cruz
725 Front Street, Suite 206
Santa Cruz, California 95060
831-459-4323
moir@cats.ucsc.edu
As of July 9, 2001

DEMOGRAPHICS

The following figures are for the 2000-2001 school year.

Grade Levels	K-12	Urban/Suburban/Rural	Rural
Student Population	19,400	**Ethnic Makeup*** African American American Indian Asian American Caucasian Filipino Hispanic Pacific Islander	0.6% 0.3% 1.2% 23.6% 1.2% 73.1% 0.1%
Teacher Population	955	**% New Teachers**	20% are teachers in their first or second year
		Per Pupil Expenditure	$5,750

* The statistics available from the district delineated the ethnic makeup as shown. There was no information about students of more than one racial heritage.

The following information was obtained from conversations and e-mail correspondence with Ellen Moir and Judy Walsh, and from the Summer 2000 Urban Initiative Partners Newsletter, Volume 2, Number 2, of the National Commission of Teaching & America's Future.

History

The Santa Cruz New Teacher Project was established in 1988.

MENTOR PROGRAM

Unique Feature of Program	Full-time release for advisors; Statewide program development and implementation	Mentoring Is/ Is Not Mandated for Certification/ Licensing	Is not mandated
Cognitive Coaching Is/ Is Not a Component	Is a component	Mentors Do/Do Not Evaluate the New Teachers With Whom They Work	Formative evaluation for planning and goal setting; not summative
Cost of Program	$5,350	Funding	State: $3,250; District: $2,100 per year per new teacher
Mentors Are Full-Time/Part-Time Teachers	Advisors are full-time. They do not have classroom teaching responsibilities.	Mentor Remuneration	Advisors receive district salary and benefits.
Program in Existence	13 years	Duration of Program for New Teachers	2 years
Higher Education Affiliation	University of California, Santa Cruz	Program Coordinators	Ellen Moir, Exec. Dir. of New Teacher Center; Wendy Baron, Assoc. Dir.

State Mandates

Is mentoring mandated for new teachers?

No.

Is mentoring part of certification or licensure?

No

Is funding provided to support the mandate?

There is no mandate. However, through its Beginning Teacher Support and Assessment (BTSA) program, California does provide $3,250 per novice teacher per year for two years for induction activities.

Goals

BTSA's goal is to support the professional development of beginning teachers.

The goal of the Santa Cruz New Teacher Project (SCNTP) is to provide one-on-one support to assist beginning teachers in moving their practice forward in relation to the California Standards for the Teaching Profession (CSTP).

Program Design

What are the components and recommended schedule of the program?

- SCNTP at the University of California, Santa Cruz operates in Santa Cruz, San Benito, North Monterey, and Santa Clara counties.
- SCNTP is a BTSA program that is aligned with the CSTP and with California content standards.
- SCNTP provides ongoing support for two years.
- Advisors meet with new teachers weekly, in and out of their classrooms. They observe, coach, and assist with planning, assessment, and effective teaching strategies for a total of about two hours a week.
- New teachers also attend a monthly seminar series that focuses on content-specific pedagogy (with a special emphasis on literacy development) that is designed around the CSTP and builds a support network and ongoing professional dialogue among beginning teachers.
- Opportunities for reflection, self-assessment, observations, curriculum planning, assessing student work, and staff development are offered throughout the year. Teachers also participate in workshops specific to issues of equity and working with English language learners.

Are there any programs that complement the mentor program?

Teachers have opportunities to attend pedagogical institutes concerned with literacy, math, and science in their individual districts and through the County Offices of Education in addition to what is offered through the Santa Cruz New Teacher Project.

Who designed the mentor program?

The SCNTP program was collaboratively designed by: the UC Santa Cruz Director of Education, Ellen Moir; student teacher supervisor, Wendy Baron; district superintendents; site administrators; curriculum specialists; and union leaders.

Who coordinates the mentor program?

Staff members of the New Teacher Center at UC Santa Cruz and Santa Cruz County Office of Education coordinate the SCNTP. The SCNTP staff includes an executive director, an associate director (.6 hours), a program director (.6 hours), a program manager (1.0 hours), two professional development coordinators, and an administrative support staff (2.25 hours).

The program is led by the UC Santa Cruz Department of Education, in collaboration with the Santa Cruz County Office of Education and more than 24 school districts in the region.

How is information communicated to shareholders?

Communication with new teachers, teacher advisors, and site administrators takes place through regular meetings, telephone, e-mail, a quarterly newsletter, workshops, publications, trainings, seminars, and a web site.

Who coordinates the integration of the mentor program with other professional development opportunities/requirements in the school/ district?

Coordination is a collaborative effort among UC Santa Cruz, participating districts, and SCNTP.

Participants

Who is served?

First- and second-year teachers are served by the program.

Is participation of new teachers voluntary or mandatory?

Participation in the project is highly encouraged and actively supported by district administration and local teacher unions.

Who provides the mentoring/induction?

SCNTP mentors, called advisors, are exemplary district teachers released to SCNTP.

What are the criteria for being an advisor?

To be an advisor, a teacher needs to:

- Be an exemplary veteran teacher with a minimum of seven years of full-time classroom experience
- Submit strong letters of recommendation
- Have strong interpersonal and communication skills
- Have extensive experience working with diverse student populations
- Have some mentoring and/or coaching experience
- Have experience in presenting and facilitating

What are the job responsibilities of the advisor?

Advisors meet weekly with new teachers in their classrooms to assist in improving their practice. They document new teacher progress and their own development as effective teacher mentors. They attend weekly staff development meetings, training workshops, and other professional development activities.

Is peer observation and coaching a requirement for advisors?

Yes, observing and coaching is required.

Do advisors have full-time classroom teaching responsibilities?

Advisors work full-time with new teachers. They are released from their regular classroom teaching positions.

How are advisors selected?

Teachers must apply to be advisors, and submit a resume and letters of recommendation. All candidates are interviewed. The appointments are for one year; the expectation is that they will serve for a minimum of two to three years, which almost all of them do.

Are advisors paid?

Advisors receive their full-time district salary and all benefits.

How are matches made between advisors and new teachers?

Elementary teachers are always assigned advisors with experience teaching at a similar level. At middle and high school levels, matches are made by subject whenever possible. New teachers also get support from a team of advisors on specific pedagogy.

Are advisors trained?

Advisors receive an initial two full days of training in foundations of mentoring. They receive training in advanced coaching and observation skills, diversity, and adult learning and presentation skills. They receive ongoing training at weekly meetings.

Who supervises advisors?

The program has an ongoing coaching component in which new advisors are paired with more senior advisors for assessment and support.

What supports are available for advisors?

Is there professional development for the advisors?

In addition to workshops and weekly meetings, advisors have opportunities to attend talks, content-specific institutes, and conferences about mentoring.

Who provides it?

SCNTP and the New Teacher Center provide professional development.

What resources are available for advisors?

- Each advisor is given $200 for professional development in addition to money offered by the program.
- A resource and materials library is available for advisor check-out.

Do advisors evaluate new teachers?

Advisors do not engage in summative evaluation of new teachers. New teachers collaborate with their advisors to develop an Individual Learning Plan (ILP) that articulates goals for professional growth and ways to achieve these goals. Areas for growth are determined through self-assessments at the beginning of the year. Assessments in the middle and end of each year inform the revisions of the ILP.

New teachers collect information that demonstrates their professional growth in relation to the California Standards for the Teaching

Profession. Advisors review this evidence and analyze new teachers' performance monthly.

New teachers also receive formal performance evaluations from their principals.

Is the advisor/new teacher relationship confidential?

Communication between the advisor and the new teacher is confidential.

What are the resources required for the program?

- Advisor training:
  Approximately 10 percent of project costs support advisory and beginning teacher training, materials, and mileage.
- New teacher orientation:
  New teachers receive a half-day orientation at least one week before teachers begin their contract year, in addition to their ongoing coaching. The cost is built into 10 percent of project costs allocated to training.
- Materials:
  Approximately 10 percent of project costs go to advisor and beginning teacher training, materials, and mileage.
- Substitutes for released time:
  $150 per new teacher; advisors are released full-time and receive their regular salary and benefits.
- Hardware and audiovisual equipment:
  The SCNTP owns an overhead projector, chart stand, tripod and video camera. Computer hardware costs are covered by 10 percent of project costs allocated to training and materials.

Funding

What are the funding sources?

- District $2,100
- State $3,250

There are two sources of funding:

- SCNTP receives $3,250 per new teacher from California's Beginning Teacher Support and Assessment program.

- Local school districts contribute $2,100 per new teacher served. The BTSA program requires matching funds for $2,000 per beginning teacher. The SCNTP, for the last eight years, has requested and received $2,100.
- SCNTP reimburses each school district for the salary and benefits of each advisor who is "on loan" to the program.

Who requests the funding?

SCNTP requests the funding.

Evaluation of Program

How is the program evaluated?

The program is evaluated annually in several ways. The BTSA Task Force carries out an extensive evaluation of each BTSA program every third year, which includes a site visit. A panel of reviewers collects and reviews evidence of how the program is meeting each of the 13 BTSA standards. In years one and two, the program undergoes an informal peer review process examining six of the BTSA program standards. All participants in the program fill out mid-year and end-of-the-year surveys. Advisors, site principals, and district administrators and other collaborators provide feedback at the year's end. Data is collected and returned to SCNTP, to be used in an annual self-assessment and improvement process.

Who sees the results?

BTSA Task Force members and project coordinators review the results of all forms of evaluation.

Recruitment, Hiring, and Retention of New Staff

How many new teachers are recruited and hired?

185 new teachers were hired in 2000–2001.

Is there any data that correlates the mentoring program with the retention of new teachers?

Retention data indicates that 94 percent of the SCNTP participants who began teaching in 1992–1993 currently remain in education; 88 percent are still teaching.

What are the indicators of program success?

The SCNTP serves new teachers in 24 school districts. The project was featured as one of six induction programs cited for excellence by the US Department of Education.

Evaluation data collected from beginning teachers and district administrators in mid-year and end-of-the-year surveys indicate a high correlation between project services and value.

LEE COUNTY SCHOOLS MODEL NEW TEACHER MENTORING PROGRAM SANFORD, NORTH CAROLINA

Lou Coggins, Director
Lee County High Schools
1708 Nash Street
Sanford, North Carolina 27330
919-776-7541, x313
lcoggins.ls@lee.k12.nc.us
As of July 9, 2001

DEMOGRAPHICS

The following figures are for the 2000-2001 school year.

Grade Levels	K-12	Urban/Suburban/Rural	Rural
Student Population	8,100	Ethnic Makeup* African American Caucasian Hispanic Other	 25% 62% 9% 4%
Teacher Population	360	% New Teachers	8%
		Per Pupil Expenditure	$5,517

* The statistics available from the district delineated the ethnic makeup as shown.
There was no information about students of more than one racial heritage.

The following information was obtained from telephone conversations and e-mail correspondence with Lou Coggins.

History

In the mid-80s, Nancy Cope and Joan Wagner, who were high school teachers, wrote a grant in order to put a mentor training program in place. They were students at North Carolina State University, and studied under Alan Reiman and Lois Thies-Sprinthall.

MENTOR PROGRAM

Unique Feature of Program	Taught by classroom teachers for classroom teachers	Mentoring Is/ Is Not Mandated for Certification/ Licensing	Is mandated
Cognitive Coaching Is/ Is Not a Component	Is a component	Mentors Do/Do Not Evaluate the New Teachers With Whom They Work	Do not evaluate
Cost of Program	$10,000	Funding	State and local
Mentors Are Full-Time/Part-Time Teachers	Full-time	Mentor Remuneration	$1000 a year for an ILT1 or 2 and $150 a year for an ILT3
Program in Existence	15 years	Duration of Program for New Teachers	3 years
Higher Education Affiliation	North Carolina State University	Program Coordinator	Lou Coggins

State Mandates

Is mentoring mandated for new teachers?

Yes.

Is mentoring part of certification or licensure?

Yes. There is performance-based licensure in the state. Each Initially Licensed Teacher (ILT) is coached by a mentor for two years. At the end of the second year, ILTs are required to submit a product to the State Department of Instruction. If the product passes, the ILT teaches a third year and is granted a continuing license. If the product does not pass, the ILT works on deficiencies during the third year and resubmits on December 15, and June 15 if necessary. Upon correcting deficiencies and resubmitting, if the product passes, the teacher is granted a continuing license.

Is funding provided to support the mandate?

Yes, the state pays mentors $1000 per year to work with novice teachers during their first two years. Third-year mentors are given $150 for working with novice teachers during their third year. Regardless of the number of novice teachers a mentor may serve during one school year, the state pays $1000.

Goal

To promote growth in novice teachers

Program Design

What are the components and recommended schedule of the program?

- The program is modeled after the one created at NC State University, which is a clinical supervision model.
- New mentors take two graduate level courses, which are taught in Lee County. Mentors work with ILTs for two years.
- There is a three-day orientation for novice teachers at the beginning of the school year. Novice teachers are introduced to the central office staff, given literature on professional organizations, meet with principals, and are provided breakfast and lunch for the first two days.
- Activities during the orientation include:
  1. Explanation of the performance-based licensure process
  2. INTASC (Interstate New Teacher Assessment and Support Consortium) standards
  3. Lesson planning
  4. Writing of Individual Growth Plans (IGPs) based on the INTASC standards
- Mentors meet with their novice teacher partners, introduce them to colleagues, and give them a school site orientation.
- There is a lead mentor at each school site, who is the contact person for the director.

Are there any programs that complement the mentor program?
No.

Who designed the mentor program?
The program was designed at North Carolina State University. Nancy Cope created the orientation in Lee County.

Program Administration

Who coordinates the mentor program?

Lou Coggins directs the program.

How is information communicated to shareholders?

There are many ways that Lou shares information, including:

- Presentations at schools in Lee County
- Presentations on topical issues, on request
- E-mail
- School courier

Who coordinates the integration of the mentor program with other professional development opportunities/requirements in the school/ district?

The program operates on its own.

Participants

Who is served?

The program is for first- and second-year teachers who are new to the profession. If teachers have a reciprocal license from another state, they are not part of this mentoring program.

Is participation of new teachers voluntary or mandatory?

Participation is mandatory.

Who provides the mentoring/induction?

Full-time classroom teachers are mentors.

What are the criteria for being a mentor?

- 5 years' experience as a teacher
- Demonstrated use of effective teaching methods
- Applicants complete a five-page application, and they need a recommendation from their principal and a colleague

What are the job responsibilities of the mentor?

Mentors promote novice teachers' reflections through cycles of assistance. A cycle includes a pre-conference, observation, and post-conference. Mentors work with ILTs at least 45 hours during the school year, and often many more hours.

Is peer observation and coaching a requirement for the mentors?

Yes, mentors do at least 3 cycles of assistance during the school year.

The goal is for novice teachers to reflect on their practice and determine their strengths and any areas needing improvement, based on the data collected during the cycles of assistance.

Do mentors have full-time classroom teaching responsibilities?

Yes, mentors are full-time teachers.

How are mentors available to participate in the program?

Mentors meet with their ILTs after school for pre- and post-observation conferences. Mentors cover each other's classes so they may do observations of their ILTs. The high school is on a 4x4 block schedule, so high school mentors often use their planning block to do observations and conferences.

How are mentors selected?

David Whitfield, the director of human resources, selects the mentors through the application process mentioned previously.

Are mentors paid?

Mentors are paid $1,000 per year by the state.

The lead mentor in each school is paid $200 for the year.

How are matches made between mentors and new teachers?

Principals match mentors and new teachers.

Are mentors trained?

Yes, mentors take two graduate courses. The first course is theory-based, and includes effective teaching strategies and a strong emphasis on active listening skills. The second course is a practicum, with cycles of assistance during pre- and post-observation conferencing, along with classroom observation. Prospective mentors write reflections about every class, the homework and the theorists studied, since research has shown that reflection is the basis of growth.

Who supervises mentors?

Lou Coggins and David Whitfield supervise the mentors.

What supports are available for mentors?

Is there professional development for the mentors?

Mentors are welcome to take either of the two graduate courses they took initially. In addition, mentors are included in all training for new teachers, to keep the mentors updated on anything being shared with the new teachers.

Who provides it?

Lou Coggins and an elementary school teacher, Beverly Suitt, teach the two graduate courses.

What resources are available for mentors?

The two graduate courses are free to mentors and there is no charge for textbooks used. In addition, there are numerous videos that are available to mentors.

Do mentors evaluate new teachers?

No, mentors do not evaluate teachers.

Is the mentor/new teacher relationship confidential?

Yes, the relationship is confidential.

What are the resources required for the program?

The only resources for the program are the books for the courses, and these are purchased by the central office administration, upon request.

Funding

What are the funding sources?

The state pays each mentor serving a novice teacher $1,000 each year. Course expenses, including instructor salaries, are paid out of state and local monies. There are no other funds for the program.

Who requests the funding?

Lou Coggins requests the purchase of the books and any other materials needed to run the program.

Evaluation of the Program

How is the program evaluated?

Participants complete a course evaluation, and novice teachers complete an evaluation on the mentor assigned to them.

Who sees the results?

The feedback from the course evaluations is compiled and sent to Alan Reiman. It is on file within the county, if anyone is interested in reading it.

Recruitment, Hiring, and Retention of New Staff

How many new teachers are recruited and hired?

27 new teachers have been hired in the 1999–2000 and 2000–2001 school years.

Is there any data that correlates the mentoring program with the retention of new teachers?

Not at this time, but the novice teachers have expressed their appreciation for the mentoring program and the assistance they have received from it.

What are the indicators of program success?

The attrition rate in Lee County is less than in neighboring counties.

The evaluations of the courses and the program have always been very positive.

Evaluations from novice teachers at the end of each year are always positive.

6

Substantial Grant-Funded Programs

The Teacher Mentor Program
Baltimore County Public Schools
Baltimore, Maryland

Systematic Teacher Excellent Preparation Project
Montana State University
Bozeman, Montana

THE TEACHER MENTOR PROGRAM,
BALTIMORE COUNTY PUBLIC SCHOOLS
BALTIMORE, MARYLAND

Mary Jacqe Marchione, Director
Arlene K. Fleischmann, Coordinator
Department of Professional Development
600 Stemmers Run Road
Baltimore, Maryland 21221
410-887-6400
mmarchione@bcps.org
As of July 9, 2001

DEMOGRAPHICS

The following figures are for the 2000-2001 school year.

Grade Levels	K-12	Urban/Suburban/Rural	Urban
Student Population	107,133	Ethnic Makeup African American American Indian Asian American Caucasian Hispanic Multiracial	 31.6% 0.5% 3.8% 61.7% 1.7% 0.7%
Teacher Population	1,046	% New Teachers	11%
		Per Pupil Expenditure	$7,067

The following information was obtained from telephone conversations and e-mail correspondence with Arlene Fleischmann, the coordinator of the program, and Mary Jacqe Marchione, the director of the program.

History

In the past three years, the Baltimore County Public Schools (BCPS) hired more than 3000 new teachers, a significant number, because of population growth and teacher attrition. To address both

MENTOR PROGRAM

Unique Feature of Program	Mentors work with new teachers who are assigned to schools with low student achievement, high teacher attrition, and a significant percentage of students participating in free and reduced meals. Program is research based and results driven.	Mentoring Is/ Is Not Mandated for Certification/ Licensing	Is not mandated
Cognitive Coaching Is/ Is Not a Component	Is a component	Mentors Do/Do Not Evaluate the New Teachers With Whom They Work	Do not evaluate
Cost of Program	$6,000,000/year	Funding	Largely a state grant, with some district money
Mentors Are Full-Time/ Part-Time Teachers	Mentors are full-time. They do not have classroom teaching responsibilities.	Mentor Remuneration	Teacher salary plus end-of-year compensation days
Program in Existence	5 years	Duration of Program for New Teachers	As recommended by administrator
Higher Education Affiliation	None	Program Coordinator	Mary Jacqe Marchione, director; Arlene Fleischmann, coordinator

this influx of inexperienced teachers and low student achievement, the district established the Teacher Mentor Program in 1996.

The primary goal of Baltimore County Public Schools is to improve student achievement. All county initiatives begin with that purpose in mind. The Teacher Mentor Program plays a significant role in promoting and analyzing teacher effectiveness in the classroom. The teacher mentor focuses on effective instruction and the impact that instruction has on student success. The program specifically targets new teachers and provides them with intensive on-site assistance from full-time mentors in the areas of instruction, curriculum, assessment, behavior management, and interpersonal communication.

State Mandates

Is mentoring mandated for new teachers?
No.

Is mentoring part of certification or licensure?
No.

Is funding provided to support the mandate?
No.

Goals

- To maximize student achievement by improving teacher effectiveness and daily instruction
- To retain capable new teachers by increasing new teacher satisfaction with their teaching experience.

Program Design

What are the components and recommended schedule of the program?
- Through the program, full-time mentors work with new teachers and provide intensive assistance in the areas of effective instruction, assessment, behavior management, and interpersonal communication as they relate to student success.
- The program is aligned with national, state, and local standards for comprehensive professional development, and it emphasizes the transfer of content and pedagogical knowledge to new teachers through continual support in the classroom.
- The program is research based and results driven.
- All mentor initiatives are focused on the impact of the program on teacher effectiveness, student achievement, and teacher retention.
- Monthly mentor-training sessions address the components of

effective instruction, including the application of new knowledge, technical skills, and interpersonal skills.

- In its third year, the Teacher Mentor Program has full-time mentors in 63 schools at all levels.

Are there any programs that complement the mentor program?

Yes, the following programs complement the mentor program:

- The Peer Coach Program
- Building and Learning Communities
- Next Steps in Professional Development Schools

Who designed the mentor program?

Mary Jacqe Marchione designed the program.

Program Administration

Who coordinates the mentor program?

Mary Jacqe Marchione is the director of the program. Arlene K. Fleischmann is the coordinator.

How is information communicated to shareholders?

Reports are provided to the State Department of Education twice annually. Data is shared with mentors and principals annually.

Who coordinates the integration of the mentor program with other professional development opportunities/requirements in the school/ district?

Mary Jacqe Marchione coordinates the integration of this program with other professional development in the county.

Participants

Who is served?

The program supports teachers who are new to the district, have five or fewer years of experience, and are assigned to schools with low student achievement, a history of high teacher attrition, and a significant percentage of students participating in free and reduced meals.

Is participation of new teachers voluntary or mandatory?

Participation in the program is voluntary and as suggested. Teachers in their third year who are untenured are required to participate in the program.

Who provides the mentoring/induction?

See below.

What are the criteria for being a mentor?

- Possession of or eligibility for Maryland Advanced Professional Certificate
- Minimum of five years recent outstanding teaching performance, modeling effective teaching, and reflecting best practices, as well as current research
- Demonstration of strong human relations skills
- Demonstration of strong computer/educational technology skills
- Availability for flexible work schedule
- Background in diverse teaching assignments

What are the job responsibilities of the mentor?

- Providing teachers with feedback on their classroom performance
- Modeling effective instructional approaches
- Conducting needs assessments to determine the type of training and resources teachers require
- Designing and implementing staff training programs
- Co-planning, team teaching, and teaching demonstration lessons
- Serving as a school-based curriculum specialist
- Conducting research as part of the problem-solving process
- Analyzing test data and other performance measures in an effort to identify promising practices
- Performing other duties as required

Is peer observation and coaching a requirement of mentors?

Yes, coaching is a part of mentoring, with emphasis on planning, observation and feedback, and assessment.

Do mentors have full-time classroom teaching responsibilities?

Mentors do not have classroom teaching responsibilities; they work full-time with new teachers.

How are mentors selected?

The selection process includes an application, two interviews, a writing sample, and references.

Are mentors paid?

Mentors are paid on the teacher salary scale, plus compensatory days.

How are matches made between mentors and new teachers?

Mentors are matched with schools, based on the needs of the school and the expertise of the mentor.

Are mentors trained?

Yes, mentors are trained as follows:

- Monthly mentor training sessions address the components of effective instruction, including the application of new knowledge, technical skills, and interpersonal skills.
- New mentors participate in supplemental training before they assume their responsibilities.

Who supervises mentors?

The mentor management team supervises mentors. Mentors are observed and evaluated according to the BCPS appraisal process. An additional evaluation checklist, developed in consultation with the Department of Research, Assessment, and Accountability, aligns the mentoring initiative with system-wide goals and the teacher evaluation form.

The school-based administration and the BCPS department of professional development collaboratively supervise the Teacher Mentor Program. The supervision is designed to make sure that what teachers learn while they are preparing to become teachers is utilized in their teaching. The following are components of the supervision: goal-setting conferences; observation and feedback; data collection and analysis; evaluation conferences; the effective use of resources; and continual support instruction, assessment, management, and communication.

What supports are available for mentors?

Is there professional development for the mentors?

Yes, there are the following professional development opportunities for mentors:

- A week of summer training highlights results-driven instruction, the characteristics of the new teacher, mentoring as a unique professional role, the Individuals with Disabilities Education Act (IDEA), reading, and performance-based assessment.
- Mentors regularly participate in study groups and networking sessions.
- Mentors attend monthly meetings as well as workshops and seminars on special topics.

Who provides it?

In addition to using county resources in the departments of professional development, curriculum and instruction, special education, and the Department of Research, Assessment and Accountability, the Teacher Mentor Program invites national researchers and consultants such as Thomas Armstrong, Fred Jones, and Mike Schmoker to make presentations during mentor-training workshops throughout the year.

What resources are available for mentors?

Mentors are provided with the *Mentor Handbook*, an annually revised volume of research and effective instructional practices, and the *Mentor Newsletter*, which updates materials and resources.

Do mentors evaluate new teachers?

Mentors do not participate in the appraisal process.

Is the mentor/new teacher relationship confidential?

Yes, the relationship is confidential.

What are the resources required for the program?

- Salaries and benefits for mentors
- Mentor training
- New-teacher orientation
- Materials
- Hardware/audiovisual equipment

Funding

What are the funding sources?

The program is largely funded by a grant from the state, with some money from the district. The $6,000,000 is used for salaries, retirements, and benefits. Various departments in the school district pool their resources and do professional development for personnel involved in many different initiatives.

Who requests the funding?

The Baltimore County Public Schools request the funding.

Evaluation of the Program

How is the program evaluated?

The program is evaluated in a variety of ways, including:

- Surveys (mentor checklists)
- Mentor journals
- Local, state, and national assessment data
- Attrition rate of teachers

Who sees the results?

The results of the evaluations are shared with:

- Maryland State Department of Education
- Superintendent's staff
- Mentor management team
- Mentors
- Principals
- Board of Education
- All constituencies through public record

Recruitment, Hiring, and Retention of New Staff

How many new teachers are recruited and hired?

3,752 new teachers have been hired during the 1997–2001 period. 115 new teachers were hired in the 2000–2001 school year.

Is there any data that correlates the mentoring program with the retention of new teachers?

In 1998–99 the average overall attrition rate was 12.5 percent. In mentor schools the attrition rate was 19.64 percent.

In mentor schools the attrition rate dropped to 10.79 percent in 2000.

What are the indicators of program success?

The goals of the BCPS Teacher Mentor Program are to improve student achievement and decrease teacher attrition in the schools that are served.

From 1996–2000, achievement data has been tracked for standardized tests (Comprehensive Test of Basic Skills—CTBS), criterion-referenced tests (Maryland Functional Tests), and statewide performance assessments (Maryland School Performance Assessment Program—MSPAP). Student achievement has improved on all of these measures in schools participating in the BCPS Teacher Mentor Program.

- In reading, students scoring on or above grade level on the CTBS increased from 68 percent in 1997 to 81.7 percent in 2000. In mathematics, students scoring on or above grade level on the CTBS increased from 68.1 percent in 1997 to 82.5 percent in 2000.

- On the 2000 Maryland Functional Tests, the percent of students meeting standards was 98.4 percent in reading, 94.7 percent in writing, and 89 percent in mathematics. This performance exceeded the state average on all three tests for 2000.

- The improved performance on the MSPAP has been noteworthy for schools involved in the BCPS Teacher Mentor Program since 1996. Schools have seen an average increase of nearly 10 percent in students meeting standards in reading and mathematics.

- Schools involved in the BCPS Teacher Mentor Program have also demonstrated improvement in teacher attrition. The attrition rate for nontenured teachers decreased from 19.64 percent in 1999 to 10.79 percent in 2000.

SYSTEMATIC TEACHER EXCELLENCE PREPARATION PROJECT
BOZEMAN, MONTANA

Elizabeth Swanson
Montana STEP Project
401 Linfield Hall, Montana State University-Bozeman
Bozeman, Montana 59717
406-994-6768
Fax: 406-994-3733
eswanson@montana.edu
step@math.montana.edu
As of July 9, 2001

DEMOGRAPHICS

The following figures are for the 2000-2001 school year.

Grade Levels	K-12	Urban/Suburban/Rural	Rural
Student Population	159,988	**Ethnic Makeup** American Indian Asian Hispanic Black Pacific Islander White	10.5% 0.8% 1.7% 0.6% 0.1% 86.2%
Teacher Population	10,280	**% New Teachers**	There are 719 new teachers in Montana, and 354 are in the target fields for STEP. Of these, 87 are in the program. 7% of the teachers in Montana are new; teachers participating in STEP are less than 1% of all the teachers in Montana.
		Per Pupil Expenditure	Varies throughout the state

NOTE: This material is based upon work supported by the National Science Foundation under Cooperative Agreement DUE 9255792.

MENTOR PROGRAM

Unique Feature of Program	Telecommunications is used for mentoring beginning mathematics, science, and elementary teachers in this large, rural state.	**Mentoring Is/ Is Not Mandated for Certification/ Licensing**	Is not mandated
Cognitive Coaching Is/ Is Not a Component	Is not a component	**Mentors Do/Do Not Evaluate the New Teachers With Whom They Work**	Do not evaluate
Cost of Program	$75,640, based on 100 participants	**Funding**	National Science Foundation Grant & State of Montana
Mentors Are Full-Time/Part-Time Teachers	Full-time	**Mentor Remuneration**	$350 per year
Program in Existence	6 years	**Duration of Program for New Teachers**	1-4 years; most stay in it for 2 years
Higher Education Affiliation	Montana State University-Bozeman	**Program Coordinator**	Elisabeth Swanson

History

The Systematic Teacher Excellence Preparation (STEP) Project is a pilot mentoring program to support beginning teachers of mathematics and science who may be the only such teacher in their district. Montana is a very large state (fourth in land mass in the nation), with a large number of school districts (455 for 900,000 people). Montana is twelfth in the nation in number of school districts, though they are third from the bottom in size of their population. Often new teachers are hired by rural school districts, and a teacher might be the only science teacher for grades 7–12.

Face-to-face meetings are very expensive in a state the size of Montana. This project implemented a system that works, given the geography of the state.

State Mandates

Is mentoring mandated for new teachers?
No.

Is mentoring part of certification or licensure?
No.

Is funding provided to support the mandate?
No.

Goals

The goal of the program is to provide ongoing professional development in standards-based teaching to mathematics and science teachers in their first four years in the profession, with emphasis on the following:

- Using curricula that integrate science, mathematics, and other subject areas
- Actively engaging students in inquiry, problem-solving, and model building
- Using specific strategies found to be effective in engaging females and minority students in mathematics and science
- Recognizing the progression in learning from concrete to abstract, providing students with ample opportunity to work with manipulatives, hands-on materials, and first-hand experiences in laboratory and field settings
- Providing regular opportunities for social interaction and group work
- Using strategies to identify and build upon students' preexisting ideas.
- Introducing real-world applications of mathematics and science
- Using appropriate technologies including graphing calculators, computer applications, telecommunications networks (e.g., Internet), and video technologies
- Using assessment techniques that are challenging, varied, and flexible, allowing students to make some choices about how best to demonstrate their learning
- Demonstrating effective management in an active classroom

- Promoting a culture in which new teachers' efforts to promote students' involvement in mathematics and science are actively supported by experienced colleagues, school administrators, parents, and other members

Program Design

What are the components and recommended schedule of the program?

- Teachers may apply for the STEP Early Career Program in their first through fourth years of teaching. They may also request to stay in longer, but usually stay in the program for two years. Approximately one third of the Early Career (EC) teachers remain in the program and become peer mentors, and then a percentage go on to become mentor teachers, thereby continuing the cycle of professional development.
- The program is telecommunications-based, matching an EC teacher with a more experienced (mentor) teacher, preferably of the same subject and specialization. Teachers use First Class Client software and the World Wide Web to access METNET through the Montana Office of Public Instruction (OPI), to communicate.
- "Conference folders" are set up online for teachers who apply to participate. These discussion groups last for eight weeks of fall and spring semesters.
- There are two opportunities a year for EC teachers and their mentors to meet in person, at the fall and spring conferences, which are held in different parts of the state to accommodate teachers' diverse locations.
- Teachers are provided with phone cards, so that they can communicate by telephone as well as online.
- EC teachers, and their mentors, are sent "survival kits" containing approximately $200 worth of materials and books in their subject area. These supplies are resources which can be incorporated into teaching and which provide a common frame of reference and discussion between the EC teacher and mentor before and after lesson implementation in the classroom.
- Occasionally teachers meet in person, or the mentor teacher visits the EC teacher's school; however, these meetings are not paid for through STEP.

Are there any programs that complement the mentor program?

- In Montana, teachers typically begin a masters program after a few years of teaching. This is a way for them to learn more about their subject area, as well as about content-specific pedagogy. At Montana State University, the MS in Science Education (MSSE) degree program is offered by faculty from eight different science departments, as well as the College of Education. Teachers choose a concentration in the science area(s) in which they need more preparation. Each course is designed to deepen teachers' expertise in science and in national standards-based teaching strategies. Two thirds of the course work is conducted on the Internet, so telecommunication is a model that works well for many of the students.

  An Internet-based MS in Mathematics Education (MSME) program is also offered by MSU. Like the MSSE program, about two thirds of MSME course work is offered on-line. Many EC teachers have entered these two graduate programs. The EC program, with its emphasis on professional development and mentoring on the Internet, gives rural and urban teachers a strong foundation for distance-based graduate work. Since many ECs are more than a half-day's drive from the nearest college campus, these masters programs are a perfect fit.

- Montana's annual teachers' conference is held in October, and approximately 32 percent of the teachers in the state attend. The STEP Project offers workshops for EC teachers, mentors, and prospective EC program participants at this conference.

- There were two three-year cycles of funding from the National Teacher Enhancement Network (NTEN) of the National Science Foundation. Through these grants, teams of MSU faculty worked with public school teachers to create more than 40 on-line courses in numerous science and mathematics areas. These courses are offered to a national audience, including numerous EC participants.

Who designed the mentor program?

The EC Mentoring Program was designed by Elisabeth Swanson and colleagues Ken Miller (MSU-Billings), John Graves (Montana science teacher), and Mike Pierre (Montana mathematics teacher) as part of a

National Science Foundation (NSF) "Collaboratives for Excellence in Teacher Preparation" (CETP) initiative. The STEP Project is one of a few grantees implementing an induction program for mathematics, science, and elementary teachers.

Program Administration

Who coordinates the mentor program?

Elisabeth Swanson is the principal investigator (PI) for the STEP grant. She co-directs the EC program with two master teachers, John Graves (science) and Yvonne Gebhardt (mathematics), who were appointed by the Montana Science Teachers Association and Montana Council of Teachers of Mathematics, respectively. In addition to the STEP Project, Elisabeth directs a statewide Science and Mathematics Resource Center (SMRC) housed at Montana State University.

How is information communicated to shareholders?

Information about the STEP Project is disseminated in a number of ways:

- A mailing in early August to all principals and superintendents in the state
- A booth at the annual statewide teachers' meeting
- Articles in newsletters of the Montana Science Teachers' Association (MSTA) and the Montana Council for the Teaching of Mathematics (MCTM)
- Articles in the *Montana Office of Public Instruction Newsletter*
- Workshops and articles in newsletters of School Administrators of Montana (SAM)
- Programs at conferences of MSTA and MCTM

Who coordinates the integration of the mentor program with other professional development opportunities/requirements in the school/ district?

The STEP Project Early Career program of professional development is not coordinated with professional development opportunities in the districts.

Participants

Who is served?

- First- through fourth-year teachers in Montana
- Teachers new to a district
- Teachers returning to the profession
- Teachers changing grade level or subject area

The STEP Project is designed for teachers in their first through fourth years of teaching. Teachers new to a district, returning to the profession, and/or changing grade level or subject area are also welcome to participate.

Is participation of new teachers voluntary or mandatory?

Participation in the STEP Project is totally voluntary, and teachers must complete a formal application process.

Who provides the mentoring/induction?

There are approximately 80 current and former trained mentor teachers throughout the state who mentor the EC teachers in the STEP Project.

What are the criteria for being a mentor?

- Teachers who have completed four years of teaching in K-12 science or mathematics
- Leadership training of some kind, e.g., in district training, professional development classes, or conferences
- Teaching assignment in mathematics, science, or elementary education with an interest in mathematics and/or science
- Agreement with STEP's goals for Best Practices

What are the job responsibilities of the mentor?

- Participate in a mentor training workshop
- Participate in 2 to 3 workshops each school year
- Be on METNET 2 to 3 times per week to interact with an assigned EC teacher and other beginning teachers and mentors
- Support the program by working to teach according to the STEP framework

Is peer observation and coaching a requirement of mentors?

Peer observation and coaching is not a component of the program, since early career teachers and their mentors are often more than 100 miles apart in this large, rural state.

Do mentors have full-time classroom teaching responsibilities?

Mentors are full-time teachers or recently retired classroom teachers.

How are mentors available to participate in the program?

School administrators allocate two release days per year for EC and mentor teachers to participate in STEP professional development activities. Apart from these release days, mentor teachers participate in the program outside of school hours.

How are mentors selected?

Mentors are selected by a steering committee composed of three to four people from MSTA, MCTM, and the co-chairs of the project.

Are mentors paid?

When the project began, funding for the EC program was higher and mentors were paid $1,000 each year. Recently, the academic year stipend has been $350, with little impact on the pool of those standing ready to mentor.

How are matches made between mentors and new teachers?

The matches are made by the steering committee and are based on similar subject area and grade assignment.

EC teachers are offered the option to change mentors at the beginning of the second year, if their needs have changed or can be better met.

Are mentors trained?

Mentors are trained in the summer or during one of the biannual EC conferences. The model is based in part on the BEST model used in Connecticut, and in part on the practical lessons learned by MSU faculty on how to provide teacher professional development and graduate coursework effectively via distance delivery. Eisenhower Grant money supported the "train the trainers" model of designing and delivering professional development to the mentors.

Who supervises mentors?

The mentors are trained, but not formally supervised.

What supports are available for mentors?

Is there professional development for the mentors?

Aside from the initial mentor training, there is no additional professional development specifically designed for mentors. Mentors do participate in on-going professional development sessions at EC conferences.

What resources are available for mentors?

Mentors receive the same "survival kit" of books and resources that the EC teachers receive. Mentors are also provided with phone cards for calls to EC teachers.

Do mentors evaluate new teachers?

Mentors do not evaluate new teachers. The mentor role is considered to be a position of support and mutual collegiality between mentor and EC teachers; the belief is that evaluation may interfere with this goal.

Is the mentor/new teacher relationship confidential?

The relationship is confidential.

What are the resources required for the program?

- Mentor training
- New-teacher orientation
- "Survival kits" of books and resources
- Stipends for co-chairs, METNET on-line discussion group facilitators and mentors
- Substitutes for released time
- Room and meals for conferences and meetings
- Travel and expense reimbursements to attend conferences
- Project director's salary, or portion related to mentoring
- Hardware/audiovisual equipment for conferences
- Mini-grants
- Phone cards

Funding

What are the funding sources?

Funding comes from grants and the state.

Funding for the program has been provided by the National Science Foundation and has been supplemented by the Science and Mathematics Resource Center at Montana State University-Bozeman, the State of Montana's METNET telecommunications system for educators, with in-kind support in the form of membership waivers from the Montana Science Teachers' Association and the Montana Council of Teachers of Mathematics.

Who requests the funding?

The EC program co-chairs and statewide steering committee.

Evaluation of the Program

How is the program evaluated?

The program has been evaluated in a number of ways:

- In-depth evaluation of the EC Program and its impact on EC teachers through site visits, case studies, and conference evaluation tools (e.g., surveys)
- A dissertation on the project completed several years ago

Who sees the results?

A steering committee composed of the three EC program co-chairs, as well as representatives appointed by the state teachers' organizations, MSTA and MCTM, was designed to review evaluation results and align the program according to participants' needs and program goals. Findings from EC program evaluation are also included in annual reports to NSF.

Recruitment, Hiring, and Retention of New Staff

How many new teachers are recruited and hired?

Approximately 150 new mathematics and science teachers are hired annually in Montana. The STEP EC program works with approximately one fourth of these new recruits each year, as well as numerous elementary teachers.

Is there any data that correlates the mentoring program with the retention of new teachers?

At the end of the third year of the program, electronic and telephone inquiries established that 96 percent of the first 120 EC teachers were still in the teaching profession.

What are the indicators of program success?

Surveys of STEP EC teachers, along with case study interviews, have consistently shown that these beginning professionals want to continue to be affiliated with the program, eventually serving as peer mentors or regular mentors themselves. To date, a dozen former ECs have made this transition from STEP early career teacher to mentor teacher.

The following quotes are taken from evaluation questionnaires and are representative of teacher comments about the STEP Early Career conferences.

- "This was a wonderful opportunity to develop hands-on teaching techniques for my class. As a new teacher the ideas presented were invaluable."
- "What a great opportunity—new ideas and lots of people to ask when I have a question."
- "Incredibly worthwhile and full of information"
- Workshops are "the best way to connect through human contact and time to visit with people going through the same thing."
- "Helpful because they [mentors at workshops] motivate teachers to revise mathematics and science curriculums to meet national standards and to integrate new content with new teaching techniques."
- "I always enjoy STEP conferences because of the insightfulness and resources made available"

A statewide survey (n=157) and case studies (n=10) demonstrated that, compared to their non-STEP counterparts, STEP EC teachers were more likely to:

- Focus on how to teach math and science most effectively, not simply what to teach
- Collaborate regularly with peers and master teachers
- Use METNET for professional networking

- Attend professional development workshops
- Design and implement multiple assessments
- Make data-based instructional decisions
- Reflect on ways to improve own teaching, and work to change these
- Incorporate national standards and the STEP framework in their classroom practice
- Engage students in active inquiry and problem solving
- Report that "reform" mathematics and science courses completed as undergraduates strengthened their teaching practices
- Employ interdisciplinary methods
- Encourage critical thinking
- Show openness to trying new teaching methods

Current and former STEP ECs responding to interviews and surveys consistently characterize the STEP Early Career program as very valuable, and many have stated that they would not have remained in teaching without STEP support.

A dissertation study of the STEP EC program provided some insights into the frequency and nature of the distance communication between ECs and their mentors. Approximately one third of the EC-mentor pairs communicated two to three times a week or more; another third of the pairs communicated between once a week and once a month, and one third less frequently. All three groups, from the frequent to the occasional communicators, rated the program's impact on their teaching highly, supporting this viewpoint with specific examples.

It may be that this telecommunications-based mentoring model works best with teachers with particular learning and mentoring styles. If so, the STEP program appears to have recruited ECs and mentors for whom distance mentoring is a good fit.

One survey asked the EC teachers if they would prefer to have a mentor from their school district or neighboring area, if one became available. Surprisingly, the majority of respondents said they preferred the anonymity of mentors who were from other communities. EC teachers felt they had already connected with teachers in their building or local area, and it was beneficial to have mentors from totally separate work environments. Their reasons for this preference included (a) their need, as untenured instructors, to be able to discuss problems frankly without worrying about confidentiality; and (b) the advantages of drawing ideas from a statewide network of mentors, not just a single local mentor. When an EC posed a question on METNET, a dozen or more experienced mentors would frequently respond!

7

Alternatively Funded Programs

University of New Mexico Teacher Induction Program and Resident Teacher Program
Albuquerque, New Mexico

Vicksburg Community Schools Teacher Mentoring Program
Vicksburg, Michigan

UNIVERSITY OF NEW MEXICO TEACHER INDUCTION PROGRAM
AND RESIDENT TEACHER PROGRAM
ALBUQUERQUE, NEW MEXICO

Ann Claunch, Elementary Program Coordinator
Jean Casey, Secondary Program Coordinator
Hokona Hall 118
Albuquerque, New Mexico 87131
505-277-7785
Fax: 505-277-2269
jhcasey@unm.edu
As of July 9, 2001

DEMOGRAPHICS
The following figures are for the 2000-2001 school year.

Grade Levels	K-12	Urban/Suburban/Rural	Urban & Rural
Student Population	86,114	**Ethnic Makeup*** African American Asian Caucasian Hispanic Native American Other	 4.7% 1.8% 42.8% 46.9% 4.0% 0.9%
Teacher Population	6,400 in 1997	% New Teachers	6%
		Per Pupil Expenditure	$5,400

* The statistics available from the district delineated the ethnic makeup as shown.
There was no information about students of more than one racial heritage.

The following information was obtained from telephone conversations and e-mail correspondence with Jean Casey, as well as taken from internal publications about the Teacher Induction Program.

History

The University of New Mexico is a big university, with a large teacher preparation program. Albuquerque is a very large school dis-

MENTOR PROGRAM

Unique Feature of Program	"No cost" program in collaboration with the university	Mentoring Is/ Is Not Mandated for Certification/ Licensing	Is mandated
Cognitive Coaching Is/ Is Not a Component	Is a component	Mentors Do/Do Not Evaluate the New Teachers With Whom They Work	Do not evaluate
Cost of Program	None	Funding	None
Mentors Are Full-Time/Part-Time Teachers	Support teachers are full-time. They do not have teaching responsibilities.	Mentor Remuneration	Their salary on the teacher scale
Program in Existence	15 years as induction; 35 years of collaborations	Duration of Program for New Teachers	1 year
Higher Education Affiliation	University of New Mexico	Program Coordinator	Jean Casey & Ann Claunch

trict. That's what prompted the development of the partnership, in the '60s, which also included several other area districts.

When the legislature required mentoring of new teachers, Keith Auger saw the exchange of services model as a way to support new teacher inductees, as well as pre-service teachers. Mentoring began in 1984 for elementary school teachers and in 1986 for secondary school teachers. It is funded uniquely and considered a "no additional cost to the district" program.

State Mandates

Is mentoring mandated for new teachers?
Yes.

Is mentoring part of certification or licensure?
Yes.

Is funding provided to support the mandate?
No.

Goals

The Teacher Induction Program helps beginning teachers bridge the gap between pre-service preparation and the early years of employment. The goals of the induction program are to:

- Enhance the development of beginning teachers, moving them toward increased competence in their first year
- Address the problems and concerns known to be common among beginning teachers
- Facilitate the development of the knowledge and skills necessary for successful teaching
- Develop job satisfaction and retain promising teachers in the profession
- Aid in integrating beginning teachers into the culture of schools, districts, and communities
- Provide opportunities for analysis of and reflection on teaching practices (rather than merely acquiring discrete teaching skills)
- Build a foundation for continued study of the teaching process

Program Design

What are the components and recommended schedule of the program?

- A partnership agreement between the Albuquerque Public Schools (APS), the Belen Consolidated School, the Rio Rancho Public Schools, the Santa Fe Public Schools, the Albuquerque Federation of Teachers, and the University of New Mexico allows for an "exchange of services" model that provides resources that support the 15-year-old program.
- Induction support services are provided one-on-one at individual school sites to approximately 500 new teachers each year.
- Support is provided by experienced teachers who are temporarily released from their regular teaching to work full time with beginning teachers.

- Support to new teachers is primarily one-to-one. Support teachers visit new teachers in their schools, working with them in and out of the classroom, before and after school, during lunch and recess, during preparation periods, in the evening and on weekends.
- Jump-Start is a two-day institute for participants in late summer to prepare for the beginning of the school year.
- Professional support topics include classroom management and discipline, instructional planning and presentation, policies and procedures, and working with parents and the community.
- Personal support topics include psychological/emotional support, stress management, time and family management, and building collegial relationships.
- The program publishes monthly newsletters—the *LINK* for elementary teachers and *TIPS* for secondary teachers.
- Approximately 20 percent of the new teachers are in a special "residency" program for teachers in which support is highly structured and coupled with intensive graduate study at the university.

Are there any programs that complement the mentor program?

The University of New Mexico Resident Teacher Program (RTP) is a structured induction program that enables participants to concurrently complete their first year of teaching and earn a Master's of Arts in Education. The program is open to highly motivated beginning teachers who hold or have completed all requirements for a New Mexico teaching license and who have minimal or no teaching experience. The fundamental components of the program include: a full-time teaching position in a participating public school district and a full-time academic program at UNM that leads to a master's degree in education. Resident teachers receive a graduate fellowship and tuition waivers in lieu of a regular teacher salary.

Sixty students become resident teachers. They receive a $13,700 fellowship, which is approximately half the average teaching salary in the districts. They do not receive the health benefits that teachers in the schools receive; they are eligible to purchase college student benefits. Their year of teaching does not count in the teachers' retirement system.

Who designed the mentor program?

Keith Auger, a retired professor from the University of New Mexico, designed a number of partnership programs between the university and the Albuquerque Public Schools. He saw the possibility of expanding it for new teacher inductees when the legislature mandated mentoring for new teachers.

Who coordinates the program?

Ann Claunch coordinates the program for elementary teachers and Jean Casey coordinates it for secondary teachers. Decisions are collaboratively made by university faculty and school district personnel.

How is information communicated to shareholders?

The Partnership Advisory Board, composed of district administrators and university faculty, communicates with shareholders about the program.

Who coordinates the integration of the mentor program with other professional development opportunities/requirements in the school/ district?

Program people collaborate about the professional development that is done in each of the districts.

Participants

Who is served?

The program is designed for teachers in their first and second years of teaching. In the 1999 school year the program supported 496 teachers. Of those, 58 were resident teachers who were enrolled in a Master's Program at UNM and who received regular, highly structured support. Another 340 teachers were considered "new to the profession" and accounted for almost 70 percent of the client load. The remaining teachers received limited support because they were new to the district or state, because of administrator requests, because a teacher made a significant change in teaching assignment or because of other unusual circumstances (as in the case of 12 teachers from Spain).

The program is designed specifically for teachers who are new to the profession and have little or no teaching experience. The characteristics and definition of clients differ somewhat for each district, depending on the needs of the district. Clients in Belen and Santa Fe include all teachers who are new to the district. The Santa Fe program includes special education as well as regular education teachers. In all districts some teachers receive support services because of unique circumstances.

Is participation of new teachers voluntary or mandatory?

Participation in the program is mandatory for all new teachers. It addresses the state requirement for mentoring.

Who provides the mentoring/induction?

Support services are provided by experienced classroom teachers released for that purpose by each district. In the 1999 school year there were 17 support teachers. Each support teacher had an average of 25 clients, including three or four resident teachers, a large number of beginning teachers, and a few experienced teachers for whom specific assistance had been requested. In Santa Fe, responsibilities for supporting new teachers are shared with four clinical supervisors and four mentor teachers who are part of the SFPS/UNM partnership. Generally speaking, the teachers who have had previous experience have an on-call relationship with the support teacher. They are visited once a month when the *LINK* (elementary) or *TIPS* (secondary) is published.

In addition, there are 9 other veteran teachers who are released by the districts to serve as clinical supervisors in UNM's pre-service teacher education program.

What are the criteria for being a support teacher?

- An experienced teacher with a minimum of five years of teaching experience in the district
- Currently working in a classroom setting
- Experienced working with adults, preferably pre-service teachers
- Knowledgeable of subject area and pedagogy
- Open to a variety of teaching styles
- Skillful both interpersonally and in communication
- Involved in continuing professional growth
- Knowledgeable of current issues and trends in education

What are the job responsibilities of the support teacher?

Support teachers assist beginning teachers by:

- Providing information about procedures, guidelines, or expectations of the school district
- Collecting, disseminating, or locating materials or other resources
- Sharing information about teaching strategies and the instruction process
- Giving guidance and suggestions for managing students
- Offering information about organizing and planning the school day
- Helping to arrange, organize or analyze the physical setting of the classroom
- Offering suggestions about conferencing and working with parents and administrators
- Providing peer support through empathic listening and shared experiences

Support teachers make determinations about which of the above would best serve each new teacher.

Is peer observation and coaching a requirement for support teachers?

Support teachers observe classes as well as videotapes, and give feedback for the purpose of goal-setting.

Do support teachers have full-time classroom teaching responsibilities?

Support teachers are released from their teaching duties for three years, on a rotating basis.

How are support teachers selected?

There is an interview process, which includes a group problem-solving exercise. The ability to work effectively and cooperatively is a major focus of the application and interview process.

Are support teachers paid?

Support teachers are paid their regular teaching salary and benefits.

How are matches made between support teachers and new teachers?

Matches are optimally made by subject at the secondary level and by grade level in the elementary schools. When exact matching of subject or grade level is not feasible, efforts are made to make matches that approximate the skills and knowledge base needed. Special educators in Albuquerque are supported by staff developers at the APS Resource Center; support teachers serving other districts are responsible for inducting special education teachers as well.

Are support teachers trained?

Support teachers receive professional development at the APS Resource Center; they have workshops, weekly seminars, study groups, and planning sessions. The focuses of some of the workshops include: effective teaching practices, effective interpersonal skills, stages of teacher development, mentoring in education, and successful induction practices. Support teachers also share articles with each other.

Who supervises support teachers?

Support teachers are supervised by the elementary and secondary school coordinators, and are supervised and evaluated according to district evaluation procedures.

Mentors develop professional development plans detailing their focus for the year, and write quarterly assessments of their progress. They write narrative assessments of their work with new teachers on a quarterly basis. Mentors receive feedback from coordinators during the year, based on criteria that are defined by the district for evaluating mentoring and leadership skills. They also meet with coordinators each week, and receive informal feedback at these meetings.

What supports are available for support teachers?

Is there professional development for the support teachers?

The following professional development is available for support teachers:

- Support teachers are trained for their new role, with an emphasis on the needs of new teachers, developing mentoring relationships, and current trends in curriculum, instruction, and school reform.
- There are weekly meetings of support teachers, chaired by Jean Casey.
- Support teachers attend conferences pertinent to their area.

- Support teachers may have six hours of tuition for UNM graduate credit waived per semester.

Who provides it?

Ann Claunch, Jean Casey, and university faculty provide the professional development training.

Do support teachers evaluate new teachers?

No. Induction support is consultative and nonevaluative. The focus of the program is assistance rather than assessment.

Is the mentor/new teacher relationship confidential?

Yes.

What are the resources required for the program?

- Support teacher/mentor training
- New teacher orientation
- Materials
- Project coordinators' salaries
- Hardware and audiovisual equipment

Funding

What are the funding sources?

The budget for the program is paid for from the total of resident teachers' salaries, which the districts give to the program, in exchange for resident teachers. The resident teachers are paid $13,700, and the remaining portion of each salary is available to pay the salaries of the supporting teachers, mentors, and coordinators of the program. Keep in mind that there are far more resident teachers than veteran teachers who are released. So, for example, if there are 58 resident teachers joining the schools at $13,700 (approximately half a teacher's salary), the remaining $13,700 per position is used to pay the salaries of the 17 mentors and some additional, full-time clinical supervision positions, also filled by classroom teachers who are released from the district.

There had been a small grant from the Corporation for Public Broadcasting.

Attempts are made to get funding from the teachers' unions and the state for food at the workshops. When this is not possible, it comes from the generosity of staff.

Who requests the funding?

The funding is given to the university from the collaborating districts.

Evaluation of the Program

How is the program evaluated?

- The program is evaluated internally. Each year the coordinators and support teachers collect feedback from new teachers and principals.
- There was a districtwide 6,000 person survey done in 1999 that found that those who participated in the university partnerships felt significantly more positive about college and professional development.
- A long-term ten-year study is currently being undertaken.

Who sees the results?

The staff sees the results and uses them for program planning.

Recruitment, Hiring, and Retention of New Staff

How many new teachers are recruited and hired?

Approximately 500 new teachers are hired each year in the four participating school districts.

Is there any data that correlates the mentoring program with the retention of new teachers?

Every one of the elementary and secondary resident teachers admitted in 1994 completed the program in 1995. None of the resident teachers who completed the program resigned or was terminated the following year in their district, compared to an estimated 19 percent attrition rate for teachers in partner districts (75 percent elementary-level attrition, 21 percent secondary-level attrition). More than 85 percent of teachers who started their careers as resident teachers were still teaching after five years; the percentage drops to 80 percent when resident teachers and Teacher Induction Program participants are combined (Fideler & Haselkorn, 1999, p. 168).

Many former resident teachers become administrators. A number of former resident teachers are National Board certified.

What are the indicators of program success?

Improved teaching and accelerated teacher growth are indicators of the success of the program.

VICKSBURG COMMUNITY SCHOOLS TEACHER MENTORING PROGRAM VICKSBURG, MICHIGAN

Pat Wilson O'Leary, Instructional Specialist
301 South Kalamazoo Avenue
Vicksburg, Michigan 49097
616-321-1038
Fax: 616-321-1055
As of July 9, 2001

DEMOGRAPHICS

The following figures are for the 1999-2000 school year.

Grade Levels	K-12	Urban/Suburban/Rural	Rural
Student Population	2,780	Ethnic Makeup* African American Asian Caucasian Hispanic Native American	 1.6% 1.2% 95.7% 1.3% 0.2%
Teacher Population	188	% New Teachers	8%
		Per Pupil Expenditure	$6,421

* The statistics available from the district delineated the ethnic makeup as shown.
There was no information about students of more than one racial heritage.

The following information was obtained from telephone conversations and e-mail correspondence with Pat Wilson O'Leary.

History

The school district was interested in providing more support for new teachers. The superintendent devised a creative way to be able to offer those professional development opportunities.

There were new teacher induction classes that began in 1997. In 1999, there was a "buddy" system with a coordinator, who called six

MENTOR PROGRAM
For the 2000-2001 school year

Unique Feature of Program	Creative funding of instructional specialists and 3-year program of coaching & coursework	Mentoring Is/ Is Not Mandated for Certification/ Licensing	Is mandated, but not for licensure
Cognitive Coaching Is/ Is Not a Component	Is a component	Mentors Do/Do Not Evaluate the New Teachers With Whom They Work	Do not evaluate
Cost of Program	$148,360 for Mentor Director and Trainer/ Co-Director's salaries and remuneration to mentors	Funding	District, creatively
Mentors Are Full-Time/ Part-Time Teachers	Mentors are full-time teachers. Instructional specialists are full-time—one teaches a course in the high school. The director doesn't have classroom teaching responsibilities.	Mentor Remuneration	$735 (average); Instructional Specialist: teacher salary; Mentor director: salary
Program in Existence	2 years	Duration of Program for New Teachers	3 years
Higher Education Affiliation	Central Michigan University and Western Michigan University	Program Coordinators	Annette Smitley & Pat Wilson O'Leary

meetings during the year for mentor support and information. In 2000, the program expanded and became more comprehensive.

State Mandates

Is mentoring mandated for new teachers?

Yes. As of 1993, Michigan State Code, Section 1526, stated that for the first three years of employment in classroom teaching, a teacher will be assigned by the school to one or more master teachers, college professors, or retired master teachers who will act as mentors. Schools will also provide 15 days of intensive staff development, above and beyond regular teacher in-service.

Is mentoring part of certification or licensure?
No. It is a district responsibility.

Is funding provided to support the mandate?
No.

Goals

The goal of professional development offered in Vicksburg is to support teachers in meeting the state requirements in ways that address the district's goals and the teachers' individual development plans (IDPs).

Program Design

What are the components and recommended schedule of the program?
This program is for teachers in their first three years in the district.

First year

- New teachers are assigned a building mentor. Mentors orient them to the building and procedures, help them prepare their room, and begin building a supportive relationship with their new teacher partner.
- Each first-year teacher meets with the principal, curriculum coordinator, and human resources director before school begins.
- First-year teachers who are new to teaching are required to attend six sessions (approximately 36 hours) of professional development. This course, called "Instructional Skills," focuses on starting school, classroom management, and instructional skills. Graduate credit is available. The course runs from July to May. Teachers who are new to the district but have taught elsewhere take a course called "Instructional Skills Refresher." When this course was first offered, 40 percent of all veteran staff participated.

- All new teachers receive the following materials:

  1. *The First Days of School* by Harry K. Wong (Author, 1998)
  2. *Transforming Classroom Grading* by Robert Marzano (ASCD, 2000)
  3. *Reflections on Teaching* journal (VCS Press, 2000)

- Course packets of approximately 250 pages of text, samples from classrooms, journal articles, and resource materials
- All new teachers, K-12, are observed by and conference with Pat Wilson O'Leary, one time each semester.
- Mentors observe their partners two times a year
- Pat will also provide demonstration lessons for any teacher who requests them.
- At the high school, teachers also work with Annette Smitley, a teacher who is released full-time (this year Annette opted to teach one class per day) to be the high school mentor. Annette observes and coaches teachers and provides help with every-day issues.
- Observations by mentors and instructional specialists are nonevaluative.

Second year

- Second-year teachers are required to attend five sessions of professional development (approximately 24 hours) that focus on the use of cooperative learning. Graduate credit is available. The course runs from July to April.
- Second-year teachers are observed by their mentors and the Instructional Specialist or the Instructional Consultant, as listed above.
- Second-year teachers receive *A Guidebook for Cooperative Learning* by Dee Dishon and Pat Wilson O'Leary (Learning Publications, 1998).

Third year

- The professional development plan for the third year is designed in consultation with the principal. An Individual Development Plan is tailored to each teaching assignment and each teacher's own strengths and areas of needed growth. Observations by Pat Wilson O'Leary, Annette Smitley, and mentors continue as described above.

Are there any programs that complement the mentor program?

Annette Smitley offers teachers instructional support by holding biweekly seminars, to which the entire K-12 staff is invited.

All K-12 staff, administrators, and secretaries are provided a journal, *Reflections on Teaching* (VCS Press, 2000). This student- and staff-designed journal is used at staff meetings and professional development sessions for personal reflections and conversation starters.

Who designed the mentor program?

Pat Wilson O'Leary, Annette Smitley, and Patricia Reeves, the superintendent, created the program, with consideration of the literature on mentor programs, personal and district experiences, and networking with other program directors and mentors.

Program Administration

Who coordinates the mentor program?

Pat and Annette coordinate the program. They are part of the Instructional Team, which also includes the superintendent, two curriculum coordinators, a research consultant, and a technology coordinator. This team supports the mentor program and makes recommendations that align with district professional development needs and initiatives.

How is information communicated to shareholders?

Pat and Annette share information with the superintendent, mentor trainees, Total Learning Council, and PIT (Principal and Instructional Team) Crew, who communicate with the shareholders in the district.

Who coordinates the integration of the mentor program with other professional development opportunities/requirements in the school/ district?

The Instructional Team coordinates the integration of this program with other professional development opportunities/requirements in the district. Some examples of those are Journaling, and Shared Leadership, Courage to Teach, Differentiated Instruction, and Software/Hardware Applications.

Participants

Who is served?

This program serves teachers in their first, second, and third year in the Vicksburg Community Schools, regardless of past experience or tenure elsewhere.

Is participation of new teachers voluntary or mandatory?

Participation of first-, second-, and third-year teachers new to the district is required.

Who provides the mentoring/induction?

Pat Wilson O'Leary and Annette Smitley mentor the new teachers, as well as the "buddy mentors" at the elementary and middle schools. Pat teaches the courses which are offered in the first and second years.

What are the criteria for being a mentor?

- Tenured
- 4+ years in the district
- Request to be a mentor
- Principal recommendation
- Agreement to attend training and carry out role
- Invitation by Pat or Annette

Is peer observation and coaching a requirement for the mentors?

Yes, first-year mentors are asked to observe, leave notes, and discuss the lesson with the mentee once per semester.

Do mentors have full-time classroom teaching responsibilities?

"Buddy mentors" have full-time teaching responsibilities. Pat is an instructional specialist, whose responsibilities relate to professional development. Annette is an instructional consultant and a teacher who is released three fourths of the time to mentor the new teachers at the high school. (Half of the high school staff is non-tenured.)

How are mentors available to participate in the program?

Mentors are released from their teaching duties for training as mentors, and are required to observe new teachers. Principals have offered to provide substitutes for mentors to observe, and Pat and Annette also cover classes.

How are mentors selected?

Mentors are selected from those who request to be a mentor, with the recommendation of the principal, Annette, and Pat.

Are mentors paid?

Mentors are paid on a sliding scale. They receive payment from an extra-duty contract.

How are matches made between mentors and new teachers?

Grade level, subject matter, location, and willingness to support new teachers are all considered in matching mentors and new teachers.

Are mentors trained?

Yes, mentors are trained at four leadership sessions (approximately 30 hours); one of these days is scheduled before the school year, and the other three are throughout the school year. Released time is provided.

Who supervises mentors?

Annette Smitley, Pat Wilson O'Leary, and principals supervise mentors.

What supports are available for mentors?

Is there professional development for the mentors?

Yes. The following are two professional development options for mentors:

- Coach-to-coach support from Annette and Pat
- College credit for the courses taken

Who provides it?

Annette and Pat train the mentors.

What resources are available for mentors?

- Substitutes are provided for three training days and time to observe.
- The district has purchased journals, books, and videotapes that are available for training sessions and to all mentors from the Professional Library.
- Mentors receive packets of materials from trainings.

Do mentors evaluate new teachers?

No, mentors do not evaluate new teachers. They support and coach them.

Is the mentor-new teacher relationship confidential?

Yes. The relationship is confidential. Some issues are discussed in mentor training as a means of supporting, instruction, and encouraging the new teacher-mentor relationship and the growth of professionalism.

Resources Required

- Mentor director's salary
- Trainer/Co-director's salary
- Remuneration to mentors
- New teacher orientation
- Materials
- Hardware/Software

Funding

Pat Wilson O'Leary's position is funded in an unusual way. She is hired by the Vicksburg Community Schools to work 210 days a year. She works approximately 75 days a year for other school systems (former clients of Pat's when she was an independent consultant), who pay her fee to the Vicksburg Community Schools. These fees offset 60 percent of Pat's salary.

The remainder of Pat's salary, Annette's salary, and other costs of the program are paid for through graduate credit tuition reimbursement, sale of VCS Press journals, and the school district's budget.

Who requests the funding?

Vicksburg Community Schools has a proposal process that goes through an administrative teacher council and the school board. Pat and Annette make a proposal through this process.

Evaluation of the Program

What is the evaluation process?

Perceptual surveys are given to new teachers and mentors. Discussion occurs among administration and staff.

Who sees the results?

The PIT Crew, Annette, Pat, mentor teachers, mentees, and the Superintendent see the results.

Recruitment, Hiring, and Retention of New Staff

How many new teachers are recruited and hired?

In the 1999–2000 school year, 30 percent of the high school teachers were new and 9 percent of K-8 teachers were new. Forty-three percent of the staff was hired between 1995 and 2000, and 32 percent was hired between 1997 and 2000.

Is there any data that correlates the mentoring program with the retention of new teachers?

In recent years, teachers left mainly to retire. According to exit interviews, the second biggest reason has been family relocation (spouse employment or desire to be near parents). Only three teachers have left the district for higher salaries in larger schools.

What are the indicators of program success?

Principals report that teachers new to VCS (first-year or veteran) who have been through Instructional Skills and Cooperative Learning are better prepared for the high expectations for classroom performance than in the past. Teachers are said to be performing with more skill and confidence by the time they have been in the district three or four years than they did in the past without the assistance.

The program goal was also to recognize capable veterans and enable them to consider new professional perspectives. These quotations from mentors' reflections are another indicator of success:

- "After I called my mentee in the summer, I found myself getting excited about the start of the school year. In talking with her,

I realized how routine start of school things had become for me and the conversation helped me understand just how far I had come in the field of education. . . . Our conferencing after an observation reminded me how important it is for new teachers (along with veterans) to get feedback not only from students, but from colleagues as well."—Jeff Briggs, 7th-grade math teacher

- "It was interesting for me to mentor someone who is older and more experienced than me. Since my mentee came from another school district, I found it very interesting to talk to him about the differences between the two districts. I really came to appreciate the student. . . . I believe that I am a better teacher for this experience."—Kim Roberts, computer education teacher

- "Being a veteran teacher can be like acting in a well-rehearsed play. When I mentor, I relive what it is like to begin again. I am energized every year by this feeling of starting over again." —Annette Smitley, high school English teacher, and now co-director of the program.

Part 3

Now What?

8

Implications for Induction

Did you find yourself envisioning a model in your district? Maybe some of the things you read about sparked ideas you would like to explore. As you consider all of the information presented, think about what you want to achieve through your induction program.

Remember that mentors can help new teachers by:

- Providing emotional support and encouragement
- Providing information about the daily working of the school and the cultural norms of the school community
- Promoting cultural proficiency regarding students and their families
- Cognitive coaching

Set the goals that you believe are important for your program. As you may have noticed in some of the models, what you are able to achieve is not necessarily a function of whether your state mandates and funds mentoring. Think about the structures that you believe will have the most impact on the success of your new teachers, and then work to find ways to make it possible.

For instance, do you want to have full- or part-time mentors? This decision is not necessarily dependent on whether you are in a state that mandates and/or funds mentoring. Your decision will reflect the nature of the experience you want for your new teachers. Do you wish to ensure that cognitive coaching will be a consistent part of the induction of new teachers? Providing opportunities for structured professional development and promoting reflection on practice require both training and time.

Six of the models—Pajaro Valley, Joint School District No. 2, Baltimore County, Vicksburg, the University of New Mexico, and Columbus—have full-time mentors. Full-time mentoring indicates a significant commitment on the part of the district to the induction of new teachers. Joint School District No. 2 is in Idaho, where mentoring is mandated and funded. The Vicksburg, Michigan, University of New Mexico, and Columbus, Ohio models are in states where mentoring is state mandated but not funded, and Baltimore County is in Maryland, where mentoring is neither mandated nor funded; these four models are funded in other ways. Pajaro Valley is in California, a state that heavily supports induction programs yet doesn't mandate mentoring.

Some districts believe that mentors/support providers need to be current classroom teachers. They have chosen to arrange for mentoring in other ways, including released time for observation and coaching. Mentors in the Rochester City School District who work with four new teachers job-share teaching assignments. Mentors in Glendale Union teach in the morning and mentor the rest of the day. The ratio of new teachers to mentors/support providers is an important consideration because it affects the amount of time available for cognitive coaching.

In the Rochester City Schools, for example, the mentors who job-share a teaching position are each devoting 50 percent of their workdays to four people. Full-time mentors/support providers who have a large group of new teachers to mentor might not see them any more frequently than part-time mentors who have fewer teachers to mentor.

Some programs have designed two levels of support providers, all of whom are full-time classroom teachers. In Aurora, there are mentors and district resource teachers; Dover-Sherborn has mentors and teacher leaders; and Saint Paul has building mentors and resource colleagues. In these models, the mentors are usually in the buildings providing frequent contact and coaching, and the district resource teachers, Teacher Leaders, and resource colleagues provide structured professional development opportunities for new teachers, as well as coordinate parts of the induction program. In Vicksburg, two instructional specialists, one of whom is also the director of the program, do the cognitive coaching and teach courses for teachers, and the mentors do the more frequent, on-site mentoring.

Mentors who are full-time teachers have to balance their response to the needs of their students and families with the needs of the new teacher. Even when districts provide substitutes for observations and cognitive coaching, the mentors may not observe as often as they think is optimal because they don't want to be out of their classrooms so much. Each mentor seeks to find a balance between all the needs he or she must meet.

Lengthening the duration of the program is another way that districts have found to increase support for new teachers' professional growth. Typically, mentor programs are designed for the new teacher's first year. However, districts are increasingly realizing the significant gains that may be made during longer periods of induction. Seven of the models presented are three-year programs: Glendale Union, Muscogee, Joint School District No. 2, Baltimore County, Vicksburg, Saint Paul, and Lee County. These districts vary significantly in terms of per pupil expenditures and funding of their programs. This variation shows how districts make important decisions about program design that reflect priorities, not just the extent of their monetary resources.

Remuneration is yet another way that districts demonstrate that they value mentoring and want to ensure that it is consistently provided to new teachers.

In the programs described, stipends for classroom teachers who are also support providers range from $200 in North Haven to $3,000 in Saint Paul.

Baltimore County, Columbus, Rochester, and Joint School District No. 2 pay the support providers additional percentages of teaching salaries. The University of New Mexico model and the Santa Cruz New Teacher Project pay teaching salaries, and Vicksburg does a combination of a salaried director/instructional specialist, a teaching salaried instructional specialist, and building mentors who are paid a stipend.

State mandates and funding are predictors of remuneration for mentors, as is evident in the fact that Connecticut has mandated and funded mentoring and pays mentors $200 at the most, and Minnesota has not mandated mentoring and pays $735 or more for mentors and support providers. Connecticut had originally funded induction much more than it currently does, so mentors are now paid, if they are paid, significantly less than they were when the BEST program was created. Efforts are under way, in Connecticut and many other states, to add or increase state funding of induction programs.

There are also very large differences in the per pupil expenditures of the districts, ranging from $4,600 to $11,000. More than one district described the extra generosity and good will of staff members in providing refreshments at meetings when there wasn't money in the program budget to purchase food. The resources available in your district may also include access to an institution of higher education, and the possibility of collaboration.

There are examples of small districts creating programs with modest grants as seed money, as well as large districts that have considered ways to address the challenges they face to support so many new teachers and the diverse needs of their students. The telecommunications model is an example of stepping out of the box to address problems that elude typical solutions. The University of New Mexico model represents a different way to fund an induction program, and exemplifies that same spirit of ingenuity. As you consider the programs described, keep your mind open to the possibilities.

The National Staff Development Council (NSDC) has recently revised its standards for staff development, and they can offer you guidance as you think about supporting new teachers with the ultimate goal of improving the learning of all students. These standards relate to context, process, and content. Many of the standards articulated are evident in the induction programs that have been presented.

For example, the context standards include the following:

- Skillful school and district leaders who guide continuous instructional improvement
- Resources to support adult learning and collaboration
- Preparation for understanding and appreciating all students; creating safe, orderly, and supportive learning environments; and maintaining high expectations for academic achievement
- Instruction on in-depth content knowledge; research-based instructional strategies to assist students in meeting rigorous academic standards; and various types of classroom assessment

The process standards include the following:

- Learning strategies appropriate to the intended goal

- Knowledge about human learning and change
- Knowledge and skills for collaboration among educators

These standards for staff development may expand your thinking as you embark on developing or enriching your program. The descriptions of the models include evidence of educators throughout the United States working toward realizing these standards in their staff development programs for new teachers.

It is equally important to consider the ways you will use to assess the effectiveness of your program. Many programs do evaluations at the end of the school year, surveying mentors, new teachers, and sometimes administrators. You may use other ways to find out if you are achieving the desired outcomes.

Are there testing requirements in your state for new teachers to move from one level of certification to another? If so, your induction program may assist teachers in becoming fully certified. For example, PRAXIS III is now a requirement in the state of Ohio. Accordingly, as mentor programs are established or expanded, consideration is given to ways to support new teachers in their endeavors to pass the test. All of the consulting teachers in the PAR program in Columbus, Ohio, are trained to administer PRAXIS III, and utilize their knowledge to inform their work with new teachers in their district. Teachers' performances on such tests may be strong indicators of the impact of the program on new teachers' growing proficiency.

Many states have defined professional standards for teachers and are also linking these standards with expectations for student learning. This is a complicated process. The California Formative Assessment and Support System for Teachers (CFASST) has been piloted as a way of linking the California Standards for the Teaching Profession and the California Student Academic Content Standards and Frameworks, and it is being used in many BTSA sites. Baltimore County has been utilizing extensive measures of student achievement and analyzing the impact of mentoring on student performance in the 63 schools in which the program is being used.

Given the commitment of time and money that any induction program will require, it is increasingly important to consider ways to ascertain if the induction programs we are creating and implementing are impacting student achievement and new teacher retention. Systems are beginning to collect teacher retention data. However, finding ways to link mentoring, teacher effectiveness, and student achievement is a more complex task. Some systems are already taking on this challenge. Learning from them is an important next step.

The educators I spoke with during the course of writing this book have been enthusiastic, and even passionate, about the necessity of induction programs for new teachers and the benefits of mentoring. Their commitment to their new colleagues has been evident as they recounted the ways they have developed and refined their programs. I have not met the majority of directors of the models described. Yet their vibrancy and zeal have been almost palpable during our telephone conversations. This degree of investment is, I believe, a key component in the success of their programs. To a person, the directors I interviewed were generous with their time and excited about sharing with you what they have developed and learned from their experiences.

More and more educators are formalizing their support of new teachers by creating programs that make explicit the expectations of the district and guide and instruct new teachers to become even more skillful. Continue to learn about other programs and approaches to induction from as many sources as possible.

Many national educational organizations have sessions on mentoring at their annual conferences. The New Teacher Project, at the University of California at Santa Cruz, hosts an annual symposium on mentoring. The Association for Supervision and Curriculum Development has a special interest group about mentoring, the Mentoring Leadership and Resource Network; its Web site is www.mentors.net.

Keep reading, share with others, and then get started.

State Mandated/Not State Mandated

Mandated	*Not Mandated*
Colorado	Arizona
Connecticut	California
Idaho	Georgia
Massachusetts	Maryland
Michigan	Minnesota
Missouri	Montana
New Mexico	New York
North Carolina	
Ohio	
Virginia	

Urban/Suburban/Rural

Urban	*Suburban*	*Rural*
Aurora, CO	Glendale Union, AZ	Pajaro Valley, CA
Joint School District No. 2, ID	Pajaro Valley, CA	Joint School District No. 2, ID
Muscogee County, GA	North Haven, CT	Vicksburg, MI
Baltimore County, MD	Muscogee County, GA	STEP, MT
Saint Paul, MN	Joint School District No. 2, ID	Lee County, NC
Albuquerque, NM	Dover-Sherborn, MA	Albuquerque, NM
Rochester City Schools, NY	Francis Howell School District, MO	
Columbus, OH		
Newport News, VA		

Student Population

Small

District	Student Population
Dover-Sherborn, MA	1,982
Vicksburg, MI	2,780
North Haven, CT	3,486
Lee County, NC	8,100
Glendale Union, AZ	13,683
Francis Howell School District, MO	18,523
Pajaro Valley, CA	19,400

Medium

District	Student Population
Joint School District No. 2, ID	24,000
Aurora, CO	28,313
Muscogee County, GA	33,000
Newport News, VA	33,000
Rochester City Schools, NY	38,000
Saint Paul, MN	46,000

Large

District	Student Population
Columbus, OH	66,000
Albuquerque, NM	86,114
Baltimore County, MD	107,133

State	Student Population
Montana	159,988

Per Pupil Expenditure

District	Per Pupil Expenditure
Joint School District No. 2, ID	4,600
Aurora, CO	4,947
Glendale Union, AZ	5,391
Albuquerque, NM	5,400
Newport News, VA	5,500
Lee County, NC	5,517
Muscogee County, GA	5,642
Francis Howell School District, MO	5,744
Pajaro Valley, CA	5,750
Vicksburg, MI	6,421
North Haven, CT Elementary and middle school	6,753
Baltimore County, MD	7,067
Columbus, OH	7,400
Dover-Sherborn, MA	7,537
North Haven, CT High school	8,338
Saint Paul, MN	9,500
Rochester City Schools, NY	11,000

NOTE: Per Pupil Expenditure information is not available for STEP in Montana.

Duration of Programs

1 Year	2 Years	3 Years
Aurora, CO	Pajaro Valley, CA	Glendale Union, AZ
Dover-Sherborn, MA	North Haven, CT (possibly 3)	Muscogee County, GA
Baltimore County, MD (as recommended by administrator)	Baltimore County, MD (as recommended by administrator)	Joint School District No. 2, ID
Francis Howell School District, MO (possibly 2)	STEP, MT (possibly 3 or 4)	Baltimore County, MD (as recommended by administrator)
University of New Mexico, NM	Lee County, NC (possibly longer)	Vicksburg, MI
Rochester City Schools, NY (possibly longer)		Saint Paul, MN
Columbus, OH (possibly 2)		
Newport News, VA (possibly 2)		

Full-Time/Part-Time Mentors

Full-Time Teacher	*Part-Time Mentor*	*Full-Time Mentor*
Aurora, CO	Glendale Union, AZ	Pajaro Valley, CA
North Haven, CT	Rochester City Schools, NY	Joint School District No. 2, ID
Muscogee County, GA		Baltimore County, MD
Joint School District No. 2, ID		Vicksburg, MI
Dover-Sherborn, MA		Lee County, NC
Vicksburg, MI		Albuquerque, NM
Saint Paul, MN		Columbus, OH
Francis Howell School District, MO		
STEP, MT		
Lee County, NC		

Monetary Remuneration for Support Providers

District	Stipend	Teaching Salary	Teaching Salary +	Salary
North Haven, CT	$200			
Aurora, CO	Mentor: $250-600; District resource teacher: $750-2,200			
Francis Howell School District, MO	$350			
STEP, MT	$350			
Muscogee County, GA	$500 or less	Director & system mentors: 11 months pro-rated		
Newport News, VA	$500			
Dover-Sherborn, MA	Mentor: $750; Teacher leaders: $1,000			
Lee County, NC	$1,000 for ILT 1 & 2; $150 for ILT 3			
Saint Paul, MN	Building mentor: $250-300; Resource colleague: $3,000			
Vicksburg, MI	Mentors: $735	Instructional specialist		Mentor director
Glendale Union, AZ		Teaching salary		
Pajaro Valley, CA		Teaching salary		
Albuquerque, NM		Teacher salary		

Monetary Remuneration for Support Providers, continued

District	Stipend	Teaching Salary	Teaching Salary +	Salary
Baltimore County, MD			Teaching salary + end of year compensation days	
Joint School District No. 2, ID	Building mentor: $200		Beginning teacher advisor: Teaching salary + 10 extra days	
Rochester City Schools, NY			Teaching salary + 5-10% base	
Columbus, OH			Teaching salary + 20% base	

9

Getting Started

You want to get started. You know about the needs of new teachers and ways that mentoring has supported them. You've familiarized yourself with the varied approaches to induction described in Part 2. Now what?

How long will it take to begin a program, or refine/enhance one? Thinking of your visit to Yellowstone, we know that some people plan the trip a year in advance, others a few months before the desired departure date, and still others take advantage of last-minute travel opportunities and may be reading the travel guide as they are flying to their destination. So it is with designing or refining a mentor program.

Ideally, take a year to form a steering committee to research and plan your program, collaborate with key shareholders, select and train key personnel including mentors, create or adapt training and orientation materials, and implement your program. Sometimes this isn't possible because you feel the urgency of doing something for the people you have just hired. In that case, you may feel as though you are hastily planting your garden without the recommended preparation of the soil and the time to tend it as thoroughly as you would like. Get started if you must, and plan on using your first year as a pilot, knowing that you will be able to devote more time next year to nourishing the soil so that even more flowers may bloom.

So what are the steps to creating or enhancing your program? What follows are recommended guidelines for you to adapt as they fit your situation. Amidst all the hard work entailed, I hope you have some fun with it. After all, what could be more gratifying than welcoming new teachers into the profession, and working together to heighten our effectiveness as teachers for the benefit of our students?

Twenty Steps Toward a Successful Mentoring Program

1. Set goals for your mentoring program. What do you want to accomplish?
2. Identify the new teachers who will be included in your program. Whom do you want to serve—beginning teachers, teachers new to your district, teachers who have changed grade level or subject area, teachers returning to the profession after being absent for several or more years?
3. Identify your resources—money, other forms of compensation, and most importantly, personnel.
4. Identify a coordinator or steering committee. Determine whether the committee is advisory or will have decision-making responsibilities.
5. Consider the models in Part 2 and determine if any of them address your goals in ways that are feasible. Continually research ways to provide professional development that supports new and veteran teachers.
6. Formulate a plan to pilot.
7. Establish a timeline for the implementation of your plan.
8. Meet with school administrators, teachers' association leadership, and the school committee or board to make the case for the program.
9. Revise your plan and timeline based on the input of the key shareholders, if necessary.
10. Communicate the beginning of your program with all school staff and the community.
11. Establish criteria and an application process to select mentors in the spring. Select extra mentors for unanticipated summer and last-minute hiring.
12. Create handbooks for mentors and new teachers that include the goals of the program, the expectations for participation by mentors and new teachers, and the schedule of meetings

and professional development activities. Including other resource materials will increase the likelihood that it will be referred to throughout the school year.

13. Train mentors/support providers.
14. Plan and offer new teacher orientation.
15. Form cohort groups of mentors and new teachers, and schedule periodic meetings throughout the school year.
16. Plan professional development for new teachers and mentors.
17. Develop ways to evaluate your program. Begin collecting data when your program starts, and collect it periodically throughout the year. Determine who will analyze the data, and how it will be communicated to the administration, staff, and larger school community.
18. Revise your program based on your analysis of the evaluations and your own perceptions.
19. Begin Year 2 with increased confidence in the fit of your program to your school district's needs and resources.
20. Honor your mentors, who are passing the torch and welcoming new colleagues into the profession, and celebrate the induction of your new teachers into your school and district communities.

Appendix A: Charts

DEMOGRAPHICS

Grade Levels		Urban/Suburban/Rural	
Student Population		Ethnic Makeup	
Teacher Population		% New Teachers	
		Per Pupil Expenditure	

MENTOR PROGRAM

Unique Feature of Program		Mentoring Is/ Is Not Mandated for Certification/ Licensing	
Cognitive Coaching Is/Is Not a Component		Mentors Do/Do Not Evaluate the New Teachers With Whom They Work	
Cost of Program		Funding	
Mentors Are Full-Time/ Part-Time Teachers		Mentor Remuneration	
Program in Existence		Duration of Program for New Teachers	
Higher Education Affiliation		Program Coordinator	

Appendix B: Questions

History

State Mandates

Is mentoring mandated for new teachers?

Is mentoring part of certification or licensure?

Is funding provided to support the mandate?

Goals

Program Design

What are the components and recommended schedule of the program?

Are there any programs that complement the mentor program?

Who designed the mentor program?

Program Administration

Who coordinates the mentor program?

How is information communicated to shareholders?

Who coordinates the integration of the mentor program with other professional development opportunities/requirements in the school/district?

Participants

Who is served?

Is participation of new teachers voluntary or mandatory?

Who provides the mentoring/induction?

What are the criteria for being a mentor?

What are the job responsibilities of the mentor?

Is peer observation and coaching a requirement for mentors?

Do mentors have full-time classroom teaching responsibilities?

How are mentors available to participate in the program?

How are mentors selected?

Are mentors paid?

How are matches made between mentors and new teachers?

Are mentors trained?

Who supervises mentors?

What supports are available for mentors?

Is there professional development for the mentors?

Who provides it?

What resources are available for mentors?

Do mentors evaluate new teachers?

Is the mentor/new teacher relationship confidential?

What are the resources required for the program?

> *Mentor training?*

> *New teacher orientation?*

> *Food for conferences and meetings?*

> *Materials?*

> *Stipends for mentors?*

> *Substitutes for released time?*

> *Project director's salary, or portion related to mentoring?*

> *Hardware/audiovisual equipment?*

Funding

What are the funding sources?

Who requests the funding?

Evaluation of the Program

How is the program evaluated?

Who sees the results?

Recruitment, Hiring, and Retention of New Staff

How many new teachers are recruited and hired?

Is there any data that correlates the mentoring program with the retention of new teachers?

What are the indicators of program success?

Appendix C:
Mentor Configurations Charts

Classroom Teacher Model

Advantanges	*Disadvantages*
There are a small number of beginning teachers for support providers to observe and work with.	It is difficult for the support provider to maintain classroom responsibilities and meet with or observe the beginning teacher. Substitutes or scheduling support is required.
The support provider is knowledgeable of site needs and issues.	Teachers who are already over-committed typically step forward to serve as support providers.
The support provider feels part of a team with other support providers at that site.	There is an expense to the district for stipends, release time, and coordination of release time.
Several veterans at the school are thinking of beginning teacher needs and issues.	
There is broader potential buy-in at the site and district level.	
There is an opportunity to model for beginning teachers in the support provider's own classroom.	
The teaching skills of the support providers are typically improved.	
Costs to the district are reduced compared to the Full-Time Release Model.	

Suggestions

Select the support providers early, and train them in the spring or summer prior to their assignment of duties. A large pool of trained support providers needs to be available so that assignments can be made a soon as the beginning teachers are hired.

Ideally, beginning teachers and their support providers meet before the school year begins to plan classroom set-up and study student rosters. It is important for their relationships to be developed as soon as possible, before the support providers become absorbed by their own classroom responsibilities.

The challenge in this model is enabling the classroom teacher to be released adequately to visit the beginning teacher. Successful programs often pool substitutes so two subs visit a typical site every week and release participating teachers for one or two periods so the team can meet during the day.

SOURCE: Adapted from Meckel, A., and Rolland, L. (2000, January/February). BTSA models for support provision. *Thrust for Educational Leadership*, 29(3), 18–20.

Classroom Teaching Plus Part-Time Release Model

Advantanges	*Disadvantages*
An increased number of beginning teachers can be served with existing trained staff.	It is difficult to manage classroom and release time schedules.
Some flexibility in scheduling is offered, depending on how or whether the teacher is job-sharing.	Classroom teachers have more beginning teachers to observe and support.
There is some increased flexibility to observe and meet during release time.	There is an expense to the district for stipends, plus more costly release time
Broader buy-in at site or district typically occurs because there are part-time release teachers and full-time classroom teachers involved in the program.	
The opportunity to model for the beginning teacher in the support provider's classroom is offered.	
Teaching skills of the support providers typically improve.	

SOURCE: Adapted from Meckel, A., and Rolland, L. (2000, January/February). BTSA models for support provision. *Thrust for Educational Leadership, 29*(3), 18–20.

Full-Time Release Model

Advantanges	*Disadvantages*
A flexible schedule without teaching duties for the support provider makes it easier to observe and meet with beginning teachers.	Support providers have more beginning teachers to support and observe than with the Classroom Teacher Model.
Work is focused on beginning teachers and their needs.	The support provider may not be as connected with site or district issues, local professional development programs and the school's curriculum.
A highly skilled group of support providers usually emerges.	Other teachers may be jealous of a few viewed as "visiting firemen."
Time is available for support provider training and on going support during the day.	Potential for buy-in decreases if the program is in the hands of a few support providers from other districts or schools.
If support providers return to the classroom, their teaching practice is typically improved.	There is a higher expense to the district of personnel and benefit costs of full-time release for veteran teachers.
There is no expense to the district for substitutes for the support provider.	"Brain drain" may occur if many veterans leave the classroom.

Suggestions:

The Full-Time Release Model also required that personnel be selected early—in the spring—for this role. If there are problems in early selection, arrangements can be made for intensive training early in the school year, because it is not necessary to have substitutes to release the support providers. Those problems also can be resolved by staggering the selection of support providers so that only a third to half are new to the program in a given year.

Another challenge with this model is having adequate meeting time with each beginning teacher, given the typical caseload of 10–15 beginning teachers. It may appear easy to observe that number of teachers in a week, but travel time between schools and varying schedules and teacher availability for conversation make it difficult to visit multiple teachers every day and have quality "prime time" with each of them. By the end of the week, it is essential to have thorough notes on each visit so as not to confuse the needs and progress of each teacher.

SOURCE: Adapted from Meckel, A., and Rolland, L. (2000, January/February). BTSA models for support provision. *Thrust for Educational Leadership*, 29(3), 18–20.

References

Bey, T. M. (1995, November). Mentorships. *Education & Urban Society* *28*(1), 11–20.

Crow, G., & Matthews, L. (1997). *Finding one's way: How mentoring can lead to dynamic leadership*. Thousand Oaks, CA: Corwin.

DeBolt, G. (1992). *Teacher induction and mentoring*. Albany: State University of New York.

Delpit, L. D. (1992). Education in multicultural society: Our future's greatest challenge. *Journal of Negro Education, 61*, 237–249.

Feiman-Nemser, S., & Rosaen, C. (1994). Guided learning from teaching: A fresh look at a familiar practice. Guiding teacher learning: Insider studies of classroom-based work with teachers (Craft Paper 94–1). East Lansing: Michigan State University, National center for Research on Teacher Learning.

Fullan, M. (1993). *Change forces: Probing the depths of educational reform*. London: RoutledgeFalmer.

Gardiner, M., Enomoto, E., & Grogan, M. (2000). *Coloring outside the lines: Mentoring women into school leadership*. Albany: State University of New York.

Gordon, S. P., & Maxey, S. (2000). *How to help beginning teachers succeed*. Alexandria, VA: Association for Supervision and Curriculum Development.

Huling-Austin, L. (1992, May/June). Research on learning to teach: Implications for teacher induction and mentoring programs. *Journal of Teacher Education, 43*(3), 173–181.

Huling-Austin, L., & Murphy, S. C. (1987, April). *Assessing the impact of teacher induction programs: Implications for program development.* Paper presented at the Annual Meeting of the American Educational Research Association. Washington, DC. (ERIC Document Reproduction Service No. ED 283 779)

Huling-Austin, L., Odell, S. J., Ishler, P., Kay, R. S., & Edelfelt, R. A. (1989). *Assisting the beginning teacher. Reston*, VA: Association of Teacher Educators.

Kram, K. (1985). *Mentoring at work: Developmental relationships in organization life.* Glenview, IL: Scott Foresman.

Moir, E. (1999). The stages of a teacher's first year. In M. Scherer (Ed.), *A better beginning: Supporting and mentoring new teachers* (pp. 19–23). Alexandria, VA: Association of Supervision and Curriculum Development.

Odell, S. A. (1990). *Mentor teacher programs.* Washington, DC: National Education Association.

Reiman, A. (1998). The role of the university in teacher learning and development: Present work and future possibilities. In R. Roth (Ed.), *The role of the university in the preparation of teachers* (pp. 241–251). London: RoutledgeFalmer.

Schlechty, P. C., & Vance, V. (1983). Recruitment, selection and retention: The shape of the teaching force. *The Elementary School Journal, 83*(4), 469–487.

Veenman, A. (1984). Perceived problems of beginning teachers. *Review of Educational Research, 54,* 143–178.

Villani, S. (1983). *Mentoring and sponsoring as ways to heighten women's career aspirations and achievement.* Unpublished doctoral dissertation, Northeastern University, Boston.

Villani, S. (1999). Mentoring new teachers: A good, strong anchor. In M. F. Hayes & I. K. Zimmerman (Eds.), *Teaching: A career, a profession* (pp. 19–25). Wellesley: Massachusetts Association for Supervision and Curriculum Development.

Weinstein, C. S. (1988). Preservice teachers' expectations about the first year of teaching. *Teaching and Teacher Education, 4,* 31–40.

Resources

Adams, G. J. (1996, Spring). Using a Cox regression model to examine voluntary teacher turnover. *Journal of Experimental Education*, *64*(3), 267–286.

Anderson, E. M., & Shannon, A. L. (1988). Toward a conceptualization of mentoring. *Journal of Teacher Education*, *39*(1), 38–42.

Beginning Teacher Support & Assessment. (1998). *Supporting beginning teachers: The principal's role*. Ventura, CA: Office of the Ventura County Superintendent of Schools.

Bey, T. M. (1990). A new knowledge base for an old practice. In T. M. Bey and T. C. Holmes (Eds.), *Mentoring: Developing successful new teachers* (pp. 51–73). Reston, VA: Association of Teacher Educators.

Bey, T. M. (1995, November). Mentorships. *Education & Urban Society*, *28*(1), 11–20.

Carruthers, J. (1993). The principles and practice of mentoring. In B. J. Caldwell & E. M. A. Carter (Eds.), *The return of the mentor: Strategies for workplace learning* (pp. 9–24). London: RoutledgeFalmer.

Cooper, M. G. (1990). Conceptual frameworks and models of assistance to new teachers. In A. U. Morey & D. S. Murphy (Eds.), *Designing programs for new teachers: The California experience* (pp. 19–25). San Francisco: Far West Laboratory for Educational Research and Development.

Costa, A., & Garmston, R. (1995). *Cognitive coaching: A foundation for renaissance schools*. Norwood, MA: Christopher-Gordon.

Crow, G., & Matthews, L. (1997). *Finding one's way: How mentoring can lead to dynamic leadership*. Thousand Oaks, CA: Corwin.

Danielson, C. (1999, Spring). Mentoring beginning teachers: The case for mentoring. *Teaching and Change, 6*(3), 251–257.

Darling-Hammond, L. (1999). *Teaching as the learning profession: Handbook of policy and practice*. San Francisco: Jossey-Bass.

Darling-Hammond, L. (1985). Valuing teachers: The making of a profession. *Teachers College Record, 87*, 205–218.

DeBolt, G. (1992). *Teacher induction and mentoring*. Albany: State University of New York.

Delpit, L. D. (1992). Education in multicultural society: Our future's greatest challenge. *Journal of Negro Education, 61*, 237–249.

Dilworth, M. E. (1989). Recruitment: The good news and the bad news on the teaching profession. In A. M. Garibaldi (Ed.), *Teacher recruitment and retention: With a special focus on minority teachers* (pp. 8–10). Washington, DC: National Education Association.

Feiman-Nemser, S. (1983). Learning to teach (Rep. No. 156). East Lansing: Michigan State University Institute for Research on Teaching.

Feiman-Nemser, S., Parker, M. B., & Zeichner, K. (1993). Are mentor teachers teacher educators? In D. McIntyre, H. Hagger, & M. Wilkin (Eds.), *Mentoring: Perspectives on school-based teacher education* (pp. 146–165). London: Kogan Page.

Feiman-Nemser, S., & Rosaen, C. (1994). Guided learning from teaching: A fresh look at a familiar practice. Guiding teacher learning: Insider studies of classroom-based work with teachers (Craft Paper 94–1). East Lansing: Michigan State University, National Center for Research on Teacher Learning.

Fideler, E., & Haselkorn, D. (1999). *Learning the ropes: Urban teacher induction programs and practices in the United States*. Belmont, MA: Recruiting New Teachers.

Fullan, M. (1993). *Change forces: Probing the depths of educational reform*. London: RoutledgeFalmer.

Gardiner, M., Enomoto, E., and Grogan, M. (2000). *Coloring outside the lines: Mentoring women into school leadership*. Albany: State University of New York.

Gold, Y. (1996). Beginning teacher support: Attrition, mentoring, and induction. In J. Sikula, T. J. Buttery, & E. Guyton (Eds.), *The handbook of research on teacher education* (2nd ed.) (pp. 548–581). New York: Macmillan.

Gordon, S. P., & Maxey, S. (2000). *How to help beginning teachers succeed.* Alexandria, VA: Association for Supervision and Curriculum Development.

Gower, R., & Saphier, J. (1997). *The skillful teacher.* Acton, MA: Research for Better Teaching, Inc.

Haberman, M. (1991). The dimensions of excellence in programs of teacher education. Paper presented at the Conference on Alternative Certification, South Padre Island, TX.

Halford, J. (1998). Easing the way for new teachers. *Educational Leadership, 55,* 33–36.

Harris, M. M., & Collay, M. P. (1990). Teacher induction in rural schools. *Journal of Staff Development, 11*(4), 44–48.

Hayes, M. F., & Zimmerman, I. K. (Eds.). (1999). *Teaching: A career, a profession.* Wellesley, MA: Massachusetts Association for Supervision and Curriculum Development.

The Holmes Group. (1986). *Tomorrow's teachers.* New York: Teachers College Press.

Howey, K. R., & Zimpher, N. L. (1991). Restructuring the education of teachers (Report prepared for the Commission on the Education of Teachers Into the 21st Century). Reston, VA: Association of Teacher Educators.

Huling-Austin, L., Odell, S. J., Ishler, P., Kay, R. S., & Edelfelt, R. A. (1989). *Assisting the beginning teacher.* Reston, VA: Association of Teacher Educators.

Huling-Austin, L., & Murphy, S. C. (1987, April). *Assessing the impact of teacher induction programs: Implications for program development.* Paper presented at the Annual Meeting of the American Educational Research Association. Washington, DC. (ERIC Document Reproduction Service No. ED 283 779)

Irvine, J. J. (1988). An analysis of the problem of the disappearing Black educator. *Elementary School Journal, 88,* 503–514.

Kestner, J. L. (1994, January/February). New teacher induction: Findings of the research and implications for minority groups. *Journal of Teacher Education, 45*(1), 39–46.

Kram, K. (1985). *Mentoring at work: Developmental relationships in organization life*. Glenview, IL: Scott Foresman.

Little, J. W. (1993). Teachers' professional development in a climate of education reform. *Educational Evaluation and Policy Analysis, 15*(2), 129–151.

Livingston, C., & Borko, H. (1989). Expert-novice differences in teaching: A cognitive analysis and implications for teacher education. *Journal of Teacher Education, 40*(4), 36–42.

Lohr, L. (1999, Spring). Assistance and review: Helping new teachers get started. *Teaching and Change, 6*(3), 295–314.

Lortie, D. C. (1975). *Schoolteacher: A sociological study.* Chicago: University of Chicago.

Loucks-Horsley, S., Hewson, P. W., Love, N., & Stiles, K. E. (1998). *Designing professional development for teachers of mathematics and science.* Thousand Oaks, CA: Corwin.

Meckel, A., & Rolland, L. (2000, January/February). BTSA models for support provision. *Thrust for Educational Leadership, 29*(3), 18–20.

Meyers, H. W., & Smith, S. (1999). Coming home—Mentoring new teachers: A school-university partnership to support the development of teachers from diverse ethnic backgrounds. *Peabody Journal of Education, 74*(2) 75–90.

Mills, H., Moore, D., & Keane, W. G. (2001, January/February). Addressing the teacher shortage: A study of successful mentoring programs in Oakland County, Michigan. *Clearing House, 74*(3), 123–127.

Moir, E. (1999). The stages of a teacher's first year. In M. Scherer (Ed.), *A better beginning: Supporting and mentoring new teachers* (pp. 19–23). Alexandria, VA: Association of Supervision and Curriculum Development.

Montero-Sieburth, M. (1989). Restructuring teachers' knowledge in urban settings. *Journal of Negro Education, 58*, 332–344.

National Commission on Teaching & America's Future (NCTAF). (1996). *What matters most: Teaching for America's future.* New York: Author.

National Commission on Teaching & America's Future. (2000, Summer). *Urban Initiative Partners Newsletter, 2*(2).

Newton, A., Bergstrom, K., Brennan, N., Dunne, K., Gilbert, C., Ibarguen, N., Perez-Selles, M., & Thomas, E. (1994). *Mentoring: A resource and training guide for educators.* Stoneham, MA: WestEd.

Odell, S. (1989). Characteristics of beginning teachers in an induction context. In J. Reinhartz (Ed.), *Teacher induction* (pp. 42-51). Washington, DC: National Education Association.

Odell, S. A. (1990). *Mentor teacher programs.* Washington, DC: National Education Association.

Odell, S. A., & Ferraro, D. P. (1992, May/June). Teacher mentoring and teacher retention. *Journal of Teacher Education, 43*(3), 200–205.

Oja, S. N. (1991). Adult development: Insights on staff development. In A. Lieberman & I. Miller (Eds.), *Staff development for education in the 90s: New demands, new realities, new perspectives.* New York: Teachers College Press.

Phillips-Jones, L. (1982). *Mentors and protégés.* New York: Arbor House.

Reiman, A. (1998). The role of the university in teacher learning and development: Present work and future possibilities. In R. Roth (Ed.), *The role of the university in the preparation of teachers* (pp. 241–251). London: RoutledgeFalmer.

Reiman, A., & Thies-Sprinthall, L. (1993, Spring). Promoting the development of mentor teachers: Theory and research programs using guided reflection. *Journal of Research and Development in Education, 26*(3), 179–185.

Reiman, A., & Thies-Sprinthall, L. (1998). *Mentoring and supervision of teacher development.* New York: Longman.

Scherer, M. (Ed.). (1999). *A better beginning: Supporting and mentoring new teachers.* Alexandria, VA: Association for Supervision and Curriculum Development.

Schlechty, P. C., & Vance, V. (1983). Recruitment, selection and retention: The shape of the teaching force. *The Elementary School Journal, 83*(4), 469–487.

Shulman, J., & Colbert, J. (1998). *The intern teacher casebook.* San Francisco: Far West Laboratory for Educational Research and Development.

Shulman, L. (1987). Knowledge and teaching: Foundations of the new reform. *Harvard Educational Review, 57*(1), 1–22.

Smithey, M. W., & Evertson, C. (1999, February). Developing a model for mentoring. *National Partnership for Excellence and Accountability in Teaching,* 1–34.

Smylie, M. (1989). Teachers' views of the effectiveness of sources of learning to teach. *Elementary School Journal, 89,* 543–548.

Sprinthall, N. A., & Thies-Sprinthall, L. (1983). The teacher as an adult learner: A cognitive-development view. In G. A. Griffin (Ed.), *Staff development eighty-second yearbook of the National Society for the Study of Education* (pp. 13–35). Chicago: University of Chicago.

Sprinthall, N. A., Thies-Sprinthall, L., & Reiman, A. J. (1996). Teacher professional development. In J. Sikula, T. J. Buttery, & E. Guyton (Eds.), *The handbook of research on teacher education* (pp. 690–703). New York: Macmillan.

Stansbury, K., & Zimmerman, J. (2000). *Designing support for beginning teachers.* San Francisco: WestEd.

Stanulis, R. N. (1994, January/February). Fading to a whisper: One mentor's story of sharing her wisdom without telling answers. *Journal of Teacher Education, 45*(1), 31–39.

Steffy, B. E., Wolfe, M., Preston, P., & Enz, B. (Eds.). (2000). *Life cycle of the career teacher.* Thousand Oaks, CA: Corwin.

Sullivan, C. G. (1992). *How to mentor in the midst of change.* Alexandria, VA: Association for Supervision and Curriculum Development.

Tetzlaff, J., & Wagstaff, I. (1999, Spring). Mentoring new teachers. *Teaching and Change, 6*(3), 284–295.

Veenman, S. (1984). Perceived problems of beginning teachers. *Review of Educational Research, 54,* 143–178.

Veenman, S. (1995, October). The training of coaching skills: An implementation study. *Educational Studies, 21*(3), 415–432.

Villani, S. (1983). *Mentoring and sponsoring as ways to heighten women's career aspirations and achievement.* Unpublished doctoral dissertation, Northeastern University, Boston.

Villani, S. (1999). Mentoring new teachers: A good, strong anchor. In M. F. Hayes & I. K Zimmerman (Eds.), *Teaching: A career, a profession* (pp. 19–25). Wellesley: Massachusetts Association for Supervision and Curriculum Development.

Weinstein, C. S. (1988). Pre-service teachers' expectations about the first year of teaching. *Teaching and Teacher Education, 4,* 31–40.

Wise, A. (1994). The coming revolution in teacher licensure: Redefining teacher preparation. *Action in Teacher Education, 16*(2), 1–13.

Wong, H., & Wong, R. (2001). What successful new teachers are taught. Available on-line: http://teachers.net/gazette/MAR01/wong.html

CORWIN
PRESS

The Corwin Press logo—a raven striding across an open book—represents the happy union of courage and learning. We are a professional-level publisher of books and journals for K-12 educators, and we are committed to creating and providing resources that embody these qualities. Corwin's motto is "Success for All Learners."